ANGEBALL

INSIGHTS & INSPIRATION

Chris McLeod

Published by Wilkinson Publishing Pty Ltd
ACN 006 042 173
PO Box 24135, Melbourne, VIC 3001, Australia
Ph: +61 3 9654 5446
enquiries@wilkinsonpublishing.com.au
www.wilkinsonpublishing.com.au

WilkinsonPublishing
wilkinsonpublishinghouse
WPBooks

© Copyright Chris McLeod 2024

All rights reserved. No part of this publication may be reproduced, stored in a retrieval system or transmitted in any form by any means without the prior permission of the copyright owner. Enquiries should be made to the publisher.

Every effort has been made to ensure that this book is free from error or omissions. However, the Publisher, the Authors, the Editor or their respective employees or agents, shall not accept responsibility for injury, loss or damage occasioned to any person acting or refraining from action as a result of material in this book whether or not such injury, loss or damage is in any way due to any negligent act or omission, breach of duty or default on the part of the Publisher, the Authors, the Editor, or their respective employees or agents

Title: ANGEBALL, Insights & Inspiration
ISBN: 9781922810656 : Printed - Paperback

Back cover photograph: Postecoglou illustrations from the mural on the walls of Nunawading City FC clubrooms, Melbourne. Photo supplied: Nick Dimitrakis, Football Operations executive NCFC.

Front and back covers depict the mural on the walls of Nunawading City FC clubrooms, Melbourne. Back cover photo shows Ange Postecoglou with the mural depicting himself, Johan Cruyff and Pep Guardiola.

Design by Michael Bannenberg. Front cover image designed using Adobe Firefly AI.

Printed and bound in Australia by Ligare Pty Ltd.

CONTENTS

To Dare Is To Do   v

1	Why Postecoglou	1
2	Buckle up, Mate	9
3	A Flying Start	16
4	Living the Dream	22
5	Reality Check	28
6	The Real Deal	36
7	Changing the Game	46
8	Coys come Alive	54
9	Coach or Manager	59
10	Ins and Outs	69
11	The Money Market	76
12	Out of Athens	84
13	Kid's Stuff	95
14	Driving Mr Puskas	105
15	A one-club player	114
16	Good, Bad, Ugly... and Good again	127
17	Meanwhile, back to Greece	135

18	Hear them Roar	143
19	Triumph then Letdown	153
20	The World Stage	160
21	Doing it for Dad	167
22	Just Managing	177
23	A Personal Perspective	188
24	C'mon Aussies	202
25	The 'Big Ange' we know	213
26	The Ange Effect	227
27	The Coaches' Coach	241
28	A Way with Words	246
29	Speaking of Ange	251
30	Earning their Spurs	263
31	Eyes on Europe	271
32	We Never Stop	276
33	The change has come	285
34	'We've got our Tottenham back'	297

| Epilogue | 305 |
| Ange, for the Record | 306 |

TO DARE IS TO DO

"Angeball has arrived: Spurs send statement in landmark win for Postecoglou."
A headline in England on 19 August 2023 shouted the news

The text: *"Postecoglou's first home game as Tottenham manager served as the perfect introduction for the Australian, whose side played with the kind of flair sorely lacking from the North Londoners in recent years."*

The "landmark win" was over one-time England and European football powerhouse Manchester United.

What is "Angeball"?

Ask Postecoglou, though it is not a word he chose – "Good question. I've tried to define it… it's football that I would want to watch. When I was growing up, I loved watching teams who were exciting. I watched the players who were exciting. I loved teams to score goals."

In Latin, the Tottenham Hotspur motto is *Audere est Facere* – "To Dare is To Do," a perfect fit for the type of football that Postecoglou brought to North London's Spurs.

On 6 June 2023 Postecoglou took charge of one of the most famous football clubs in the world, the first Australian to take a top job in the most prestigious football competition, the England Premier League.

Ever since as a five-year-old in 1970 when he arrived in Australia from Greece with his family, football (soccer) has been at the centre of his life.

In Australia, Postecoglou played and coached at the highest level.

But his destiny was coaching, right from the tender age of 12 when he mapped out a championship campaign for his high school team in Prahan.

In the clubrooms of Melbourne suburban club Nunawading FC, Postecoglou's image is featured in a mural alongside those of two greats in world football, Johan Cruyff and Pep Guardiola.

The mural was painted in 2022 and Postecoglou, then in charge of Celtic in Scotland, already was tipped for greatness by those who knew him. Was the writing on the wall then that he would find himself in charge some day of one of the "Big Six" in the EPL?

Spaniard Pep Guardiola is a manager and former player, in charge of English Premier League champions Manchester City. He was a defensive midfielder who usually played in a deep playmaker's role. As a manager, his tactics include playing out from the back, ball retention, width, creativity and pressing – things he learned from his one-time coach Johan Cruyff. Cruyff was a Dutch footballer and coach who revolutionised the game with the idea of "total football," a fluid style of play allowing any player to push forward as another slotted in to cover for him.

Today's Angeball could well be based on those styles, but at "next level."

It would be a stretch to say Postecoglou's methods replicate exactly those of Guardiola and Cruyff, but just as their teams were great entertainers, the same is being said of Postecoglou's Spurs who grabbed the attention of fans and pundits alike in season 2023-24.

What was widely thought to be a season of transition and rebuilding became something more promising; a possible Top 5 or 7 finish and a return to European football were real possibilities as the season progressed.

The diehard COYS (Come On You Spurs) supporters were enthusiastic about Angeball. Showbiz identities Henry Winkler, Sir Kenneth Branagh, Robbie Williams and Dave Clark were on board, too.

Other EPL coaches were impressed; Guardiola at Manchester City and Arteta at Arsenal praised the Spurs approach.

Other football codes also wanted to learn about Angeball; coaches from Australian NRL and AFL clubs and even a coach from America's NFL all paid a visit to Tottenham Hotspur. They left impressed.

Back in Australia, those who knew Postecoglou well were not surprised at all by his appearance in the top-flight of world football.

He had an enviable career, even before he got off to a flying start as head coach/manager at Tottenham Hotspur in the EPL in 2023.

His first coaching gig was at South Melbourne, Australia, which hadn't won a league title in seven years. He guided the team to consecutive National Soccer League (NSL) titles in 1997-98, ending a seven-year drought, and again in 1998-99 as well as winning the 1999 Oceania Club Championship.

Later at Brisbane in Australia's top-flight A-League, in which the Roar had never won a title, Postecoglou won three in succession that included a record 36-matches unbeaten run from September 2010 to November 2011.

As Australian coach, his team won an Asian Cup, the country's first – and still only – significant international trophy, in 2015. He qualified the Socceroos for the 2018 World Cup.

Postecoglou then went to Yokohama F. Marinos in Japan which hadn't won anything significant in 15 years. He won the J-League championship in 2019.

Next port of call, Scotland where he took Celtic to the Scottish Premiership after also winning the Scottish League Cup in his first year there. He repeated the double in his second year then added the Scottish Cup to his resume in his last match in charge. His record there from 2021-23 included a 38-match unbeaten Scottish Premiership run for a total of five trophies during his tenure.

The elite 20-team EPL beckoned. Specifically, Tottenham Hotspur.

Not to put too fine a point on it, Tottenham Hotspur was a broken team when Postecoglou arrived in June 2023. It was bad enough that the underachieving Spurs, a.k.a. the Lilywhites (for their main-strip colour), had finished eighth. But that also cost them the chance of putting any European football in their diary for the new season.

In 2023, dreams of a return to Europe may have been secondary to many fans, but the club's history there was not forgotten. Spurs were the first team to win the UEFA Cup (1971) and were the first British team to win a major European trophy, the European Cup Winners' Cup in 1963.

To be missing from all European competition in 2023-24 was a sad indictment of the events of season 2022-23; for the first time since 2009-10, Tottenham Hotspur was not competing in any European competition.

Spurs had qualified for UEFA (the Union of European Football Associations) competitions every season from 2010 to 2022.

High on priorities for Europe was the Champions League. That would need a Top-4 EPL finish. Even getting into the second or third tier European play-offs would bring some cheer to the club.

Postecoglou's take on European football: "Not being part of it this year has hurt us because it gives you a chance to develop your squad even quicker with the experiences they have and the ability to give more game time to your squad, so it's hurt us this year."

If there was to be an upside in missing out on European competition it was that the stress (injury risk) on players turning out mid-week as well as weekends was greatly reduced.

Could Postecoglou add his name to the Who's Who of great Premier League coaches? Sir Alex Ferguson, Jose Mourinho, Pepe Guardiola, Sam Allardyce, Arsene Wagner, Mark Hughes, Harry Redknapp, Roy Hodgson?

The Australian started work on 1 July 2023. The first round of the EPL season was on 11 August and he didn't really know what his team on the pitch would look like.

By the time he arrived at North London (N17), he had coached for more than 27 years at elite level in 570 matches, from Australia to Scotland via Greece and Japan. In those 570 matches his teams scored 701 goals at an average of 1.22 per match.

By February 2024, barely six months after he started work in the English Premier League, fans of Postecoglou's Spurs were beginning to dream of what could be, come season's end in May 2024. They were comfortably inside the top 5 and within reach of top spot.

For Australian fans of Postecoglou and Tottenham Hotspur there was great hope that reports of a "coming home" visit after the end of the Premier League season in May 2024 would become reality. The plan was for Postecoglou's Spurs to play the A-Leagues All Stars in a "friendly" at Melbourne's iconic MCG.

A championship title in Postecoglou's first year at the helm of Spurs would have been extraordinarily optimistic. There were even doubters that Angeball was sustainable, particularly when his squad became decimated by injury and international duty.

But Angeball continued to thrive. Players warmed to the system. Those who seemed to be going nowhere under previous set-ups were now finding their feet. Others were sent out to other clubs to get match experience instead of warming the Spurs bench. It was about getting them ready for the future.

Postecoglou didn't promise miracles in year one, though many fans thought they were witnessing one when Spurs appeared on the top of the ladder at one point in 2023.

It was dreamtime alright.

One football fan set others straight in a Spurs social media post in December: "Even with the appointment of Big Ange, did the fans seriously think he was some sort of miracle worker? Did you honestly believe that he would turn a s… show of a squad into PL Champions or Cup Winners within a couple of months? If you did, you really are deluded!"

And another social media home-truth: "Ange was always going to need 2 or 3 transfer windows to get the team the way he wants it. He has his ideas on how to play the game, and being negative or defensive just isn't in his mantra… have a bit of faith and… be realistic! It was always going to be a long-term project while Ange gets all his pieces in to place!"

GLAD ALL OVER

In shades of a song from Tottenham-born Dave Clark of The Dave Clark Five, the fans were feeling "glad all over." Sadly for the band, Spurs didn't adopt the 1964 hit song as their own.

"I'm very flattered, but the one disappointment in my career is that I would have loved it to have been Spurs. But they never picked it up," lifelong Spurs fan Clark said when discussing how Crystal Palace chose "Glad All Over" as their theme song.

Dave Clark's thumping drums were the foundation of what became the "Tottenham Sound." Clark's first venture into the music world was a skiffle band he formed in Tottenham to raise funds so a football team he formed could travel to The Netherlands.

Dave Clark in fact tried to buy Spurs in the 60s for a million pounds. However, the family who owned the club at the time, the Richardsons, did not want to sell.

While Clark was a Spurs fan, Postecoglou also had his admirers in the music industry when he was at Celtic.

During his Australian tour in March 2023 Sir Rod Stewart had an image of Postecoglou (who was still at Celtic then) on his backdrop as he performed *You're In My Heart*. Stewart is a Celtic fan and suggested in a radio interview in Melbourne he'd even like to visit Postecoglou's old home.

CHAPTER 1
WHY POSTECOGLOU?

At his first Press Conference at Tottenham Hotspur, on 11 July 2023, Postecoglou faced a stark reality pointed out by a reporter: the club hadn't won a major trophy for almost 16 years!

"You've painted a pretty bleak picture. I was excited about this role!" Postecoglou joked.

"But to be fair, that's why I'm here. That's what I love about it, all those things that are not here. And that's what I want to bring. I want to bring success, bring European football. I want this club to be where it deserves to be."

Asked if he had to re-program the squad to play differently, Postecoglou said: "Yeah, absolutely … if it was just me rolling up and they're (already) doing their thing, it wouldn't excite me. That's part of the challenge, it will be a shift from the way the club has played for three or four years."

While attention quickly focused on what Postecoglou began achieving at Spurs, it was worth noting what was happening in some of his old stamping grounds.

Was Angeball surviving?

His most recent team, Celtic, finished 2023 on top of the Scottish Premier League ladder. Northern Irishman Brendan Rogers took over from Postecoglou having previously been in the role from 2016-19 before moving to Leicester City in England.

Yokohama F. Marinos, under the stewardship of Australian Kevin Muscat (who had been an assistant to Postecoglou there) was second in the J-League after 34 rounds. Muscat moved on for 2024, to Shanghai Port in the Chinese Super League. Another former Socceroo, Harry Kewell, an assistant coach at Celtic under Postecoglou, replaced him.

Going back even further along Postecoglou's coaching path, Melbourne Victory (now coached by Tony Popovic, a former Socceroo, former assistant to Postecoglou with the national team and one-time an assistant coach at Crystal Palace) had lost only one match after 17 rounds.

Postecoglou would not have been happy to see Brisbane Roar where he had great success sitting 7th in the A-League, conceding 8 goals in a loss at the end of December 2023, a week after coach Ross Aloisi (a former Socceroo and assistant to Postecoglou with the Socceroos) left for a post with Shanghai Port to join Kevin Muscat.

At Postecoglou's first club, South Melbourne FC where he had been player and coach, the news in 2023 was all good. The Club was sitting second in the NPL Vic Men's League and had won a place in the new National Second Tier Men's competition as one of eight foundation clubs. The competition was starting in March/April 2025.

Antonio Conte departed Tottenham Hotspur in March 2023, after taking over from Nuno Espirito Santo less than halfway through the 2021-22 season.

The 2022-23 EPL season began well for Spurs who were unbeaten in their first seven games and had 23 points after 10 rounds.

The start under Italian Conte who had joined from Inter Milan had been Spurs' best for a decade. In the 2011-12 season, Spurs under Harry Redknapp had 22 points from their opening 10 fixtures.

Spurs also were contesting the FA Cup, EFL Cup and UEFA Champions League. The future looked bright.

Come the end of the season, Conte had moved on. And Spurs finished the lowest down the ladder they'd been since 2008. What went wrong?

October-November in 2022 saw a form slump where losses outnumbered wins 13 to 11 in the last 28 games (4 draws).

Off the field, Conte was affected by health issues, of his own and among some close friends. He underwent gallbladder surgery.

The speculation was that he wouldn't renew his contract for

the 2023-24 season in any event.

Conte's final game in charge came against Southampton, when Spurs seemed to switch-off when in front and allowed Southampton to snatch a point. (That's something Postecoglou would not tolerate – he'd go "ballistic" is how one player put it.)

Conte didn't hold back in his press conference after the match, unloading on the players, the club and culture.

"We are 11 players that go into the pitch," Conte said. "I see selfish players, I see players that don't want to help each other and don't put their heart (in it).

"Being a team, it is the most important thing. To understand that we play for the badge. We have to play to make our fans proud of us. We have to play to show desire. The fire in your eyes to win. If you have this, for sure, you don't go out in FA Cup. Today you win.

"Here we're used to it for a long time. The club has the responsibility for the transfer market, every coach that stayed here has the responsibility. And the players? The players? Where are the players?

"In my experience, I can tell you that if you want to be competitive, if you want to fight, you have to improve this aspect. And this aspect, I can tell you, in this moment is really, really low. And I see only 11 players that play for themselves."

Another Italian, Cristian Stellini, took charge while Conte had surgery and was in the hotseat again after Conte's departure with Ryan Mason his assistant. That ended in tears, too, Mason seeing out the season in place of Stellini. Mason began his playing career at Spurs in 2008, ending at Hull City in 2018. He began his coaching career as an assistant at Spurs in 2021

At season's end and with just three months until the new season, Tottenham Hotspur needed a new boss.

Some big names were bandied about: Barcelona manager Luis Enrique and ex-Bayern Munich manager Julian Nagelsmann, Roberto De Zerbi or even the return of Mauricio Pochettino from Chelsea in the EPL.

Pochettino was still in the mind of long-term Spurs supporters. They'd delighted in the flare his team showed when he got them what is still their best EPL finish in 2016-17 (second) and to the Champions League final in 2019. But he went on to win just three league games in the first half of the next season, and only six of his last 24.

Australian Postecoglou from Celtic was definitely a left-field candidate. After all, he didn't have coaching experience in any of the top five European leagues which had long seemed to be a qualification for the EPL.

Spurs were going to break the mould. Chairman Daniel Levy had said the past strategy in recruiting managers had been based on "let's bring in a trophy manager."

This was done unsuccessfully twice with recent appointments (Mourinho and Conte, who'd both had Premier League success). "You have to learn from the mistakes," Levy said.

Why Postecoglou this time? Surely getting a trophy was paramount.

Levy told a fans forum: "Actually it was very easy, because Ange I would say is just a normal bloke and it was wonderful to be able to have a conversation with him where we could talk about anything and he was very direct and honest.

"I like someone who just tells me as it is, no one that plays games, no one that says one thing to me and then one thing to someone else. This club needed to go back to its roots.

"Honestly, there was a lot of pressure on me to bring in somebody that was a big name. I just wanted somebody who understood our DNA, would play attacking football, that would give young players a chance, believe in the academy, would build a relationship with the fans and understand the resources that we have and don't have as a club, and be part of a team. Ange, I have to say, is a breath of fresh air."

Postecoglou's take on why he was at Spurs: "If you want to change, you have to change.

"Unless I change things – personnel or staff or manner of playing – then what am I doing? I'm definitely not that arrogant to think that just me walking in is going to give us success. You have to actually make meaningful change. That's what the club wanted. By appointing me, I presume they wanted to go in a different direction.

"What I tried to do, from the first day they (the players)

walked in here, is to show them that it's a different place and give them the opportunity to see whether that helps them get to a good place in terms of their own confidence and own self-belief.

"Coming into this year, I didn't want anybody carrying the baggage or the burden of what's gone on in the past. There's no point in that. I don't (do that). I come in with the energy that it's something new and an exciting opportunity and that's what I want the players to feel like."

Such was the impression Postecoglou made in his first month in charge of Tottenham Hotspur that he was voted the English Premier League "Manager of the Month" for August. New signing James Maddison was named EPL Player of the Month.

Spurs marched onwards and upwards in September. Postecoglou was named Manager of the Month again. Spurs captain Son Heung-min was named EPL player of the month.

Postecoglou wasn't done. He was named Manager of the Month again for October, the first time in history a manager had won the award in each of his first three months in the Premier League.

The Angeball story had just begun.

MUTUAL RESPECT

Mauricio Pochettino was in charge of Spurs from 2014 to 2019 when they were regular EPL top-four contenders and took them to their first Champions League final in 2019 when they were runners-up to fellow England club Liverpool.

Spurs didn't fare well after that and Argentine Pochettino was moved on in November 2019, eventually taking over at Paris St Germain in 2021 before moving to Chelsea in the EPL in July 2023, around the same time as Postecoglou arrived at Spurs.

The former Spurs boss and current incumbent met in Round 11 of the EPL on 6 November, at Tottenham. Pochettino had the last laugh.

Pochettino knew what he'd be up against.

"They are doing a fantastic job, Ange and the coaching staff I know very well," he said before the game. "Very good players, very good team."

There was some mutual admiration.

Postecoglou praised the job Pochettino had done while at Spurs. "It's undoubted that he had an unbelievable impact on this football club," he said.

"All of us, in our roles, that's our ultimate goal and ambition. Whatever doors we go through we make an impact.

"And he had an undeniable impact on this football club. He almost took this club to the ultimate.

"His work is unquestioned."

CHAPTER 2
BUCKLE UP, MATE

Postecoglou quickly became known around Tottenham Hotspur as "Big Ange" just as he is known to many of his mates. As you'd expect from an Aussie, "mate" is a word he uses a lot.

His confidence in what he is doing is unshakeable, also just as you'd expect from an Aussie, even one a long way from home.

Before his first match in charge of Celtic in the Scottish League in 2021 he set a reporter straight when asked if he knew anything about his team's opponents: "I'm still on the same planet mate, I haven't come from outer space."

Indeed, Postecoglou was well aware of Scottish football, as former South Melbourne teammate and fellow defender Steve Blair pointed out to Celticway.com.

Blair, himself Scotland born (1961) and a lifelong Celtic supporter, said even though South Melbourne Hellas where Postecoglou began his football odyssey was founded by Greek migrants, Scottish ex-pats had figured prominently on the club's playing lists.

Postecoglou visited Scotland with Blair in the 1980s,

checking out Celtic, Rangers, Aberdeen, Dundee United, Hearts and Hibernian as part of part of Postecoglou's "learning and footballing education."

Two years after arriving at Celtic, Postecoglou was enjoying life as the Spurs boss or "gaffer", the term used by many in the UK – "There's no place on earth I would rather be than right here in this minute trying to bring success to one of the biggest football clubs in the world," he said.

His tip for Spurs fans? "Buckle up. It's not going to be smooth. It never is in my first years. That's not to say you can't be successful but there will be some turbulence there. I've said already that the fans are going to be my biggest barometer as to how we're going."

Wherever he was, Postecoglou motivated, encouraged and, when necessary, criticised. Above all, he inspired his players.

Case-in-point: Tottenham's Mali international Yves Bissouma, 27, was one of the "finds of the season" as the EPL paused in November for a break for international matches. Bissouma put his transformation from the previous season down to the arrival of Big Ange. "Yes, it's a very, very big reason. It's a very big reason," he said in an interview with SpursPlay. " You should know that six months before the end of last season I had already prepared for this season, because I am a fighter and I won't accept a situation if it remains negative. I take full responsibility when it's time to work to change things.

"So when I was injured, at the end of last season I was already preparing for this one, right? So I came in, there was a new coach. We see football the same way.

"He talks to me before training, he gives me all his trust, he explains (things). After that it's up to me to do things well. You have a coach who understands football, who tries to talk to you as well. It felt so nice. It has been a long time since anyone said anything to me."

In January 2024 when Spurs set about creating depth in their squad through the European summer transfer window, new recruit Timo Werner said a chat with Postecoglou told him he "needed" to join Tottenham.

"A lot of things attracted me here – first of all, the talk with the manager," Werner told the Spurs website.

"He gave me, straight away, the feeling I need to join – it's what I want to feel when I talk to a manager.

"Also the tactics and the style, how he wants to play, how he lets the team play. For me, I thought straight away that it fits perfectly. The stadium, the team – we have some very good players– all of it was very interesting to me."

For Postecoglou, the process is simple.

"With Timo too and any player I've signed, it's just a conversation about what I believe and my thoughts on them as players, where I see them fitting in." he said.

"And trying to create a picture in their heads about what they'll encounter when they get here and what we're trying to build and the rest is up to them.

"Part of the key for me is they want to come to this football club. I'm not going to bend their arm or try to convince them. Part of it is them getting excited about having to come to us."

Postecoglou operates in a no-bull…t zone. No management-speak that had become so common in the elite league. No rants in his press conferences where everyone is "mate." But if there's a proposition put to him that he doesn't like, the questioner will be met with an ice-cold stare that he/she won't forget in a hurry.

Those who know him outside the game say he's quiet, humble, honest. On the sidelines he's demonstrative, vocal and sometimes just a little bit frightening.

He strongly believes in what he wants from his players and how to go get it.

"What won't change are the basic underlying principles that I want my team to play football that scares the life out of every opposition. That's the end game," he said as he stepped into the EPL coaching limelight.

Players got on board with Angeball right from day one, breaking free of the conservative mindsets that seemed to have shackled attacking flair for years.

Spurs were always going to be treading on broken glass with their squad list. Captain and goal glutton Harry Kane was going to Bayern Munich. Other players had to step up to produce the Angeball that Postecoglou was demanding. Any injuries to his playmakers could be (and indeed was) destructive.

Some new recruits in 2023 – James Maddison, Dejan Kulusevski, Pedro Porro, Manor Solomon and keeper Guglielmo Vicario – seemed to settle into Angeball comfortably, with South Korean Son Heung-min new to the leadership role and the focal point up front.

But the loss of any of them – or any other key players – to injury or even suspension would have a major impact. There just wasn't a depth of talent available to replace like-with-like.

As the season progressed through the last half of 2023, the depth problems became painfully obvious; some of the fit players in the squad were found wanting when left to carry a much bigger burden through all the injury woes.

Son weighed in after a loss to West Ham in November 2023: "We lost the game. It is unacceptable. You are winning. Losing that game I think is unacceptable. As a player (we) should take responsibility… Attacking players should feel responsible because we had chances to kill the game. I know it is very sad for the fans and they are disappointed. As a group, we want to bounce back as soon as possible."

Postecoglou also was stung by the loss to West Ham: "It's another game where we've dominated the game and we haven't turned that dominance into something more tangible," he said.

"Us being good means us being 3-0 up. I try to set up teams to win games. 1-0 at half-time was not a good performance.

"We're playing so-called good football, but I see us not

showing any clear conviction in what we're doing. It's almost like we hope the ball will go into the net by itself.

"We've played some decent football, great. But ultimately, we play to try to win games not to just put on a show."

The club's worst fears had been realised a few weeks earlier when recruits Maddison and van de Ven were ruled out until early 2024 through serious injuries. Maddison missed three months and van de Ven almost two months.

As one commentator noted at year's end, Spurs were "running on fumes."

A critical point came in the 4-1 loss to Chelsea that produced the injuries and send-offs (two) that the club probably always feared would bite it at some stage, though not all at once.

Spurs' best start in top-flight competition since 1960 ended abruptly. Until the Chelsea game, Spurs hadn't lost a game in 10 rounds (eight wins and two draws). A concern was also developing as the season progressed into 2024 that Spurs were conceding goals late in the game – eight times in the 90th minute, more than any other team.

Postecoglou's first three months were unquestionably successful. He'd become the first person to win the Premier League Manager of the Month award in all first three months in charge.

He copped criticism from some pundits after the loss to Chelsea. He was being "naïve" and even "arrogant" by not throwing everyone into defence when the team was down to nine men, someone said. Suffice to say, most of the criticism came from those whose name was preceded by "former" or those who hadn't been paying attention when from the beginning Postecoglou promised attacking football.

Most fans were happy to see their side continuing to attack from the deep. They stood and cheered their team off the pitch at the end of the Chelsea game.

Postecoglou saw a positive: "Disappointed by the result but really proud of the players, they gave everything and that is the positive we will take," he said.

"It might take a little while, but we'll get through it and as long as we show the same intent and play the football we did today I've got no doubt when we come out the other side, we'll be a very good football team."

An upside in three successive losses that pushed the side out of the top four was that they'd scored first in each game. And even down to nine players against Chelsea, Spurs continued to get a good share of possession (39%) and in losses to Wolves and Villa they actually dominated possession (58.5% and 62% respectively).

The stats for each match told the story. Spurs dominated possession, shots on goal and passes in almost all of them. They just didn't get the ball in the net at crucial times.

CHAPTER 3
A FLYING START

Spurs showed plenty of promise in the first half of their new season under Postecoglou's guidance.

The Australian made the best start of any new manager in Premier League history.

The first 9 games from 13 August told the story: 23 points; most shots on goal; most shots on target; most final-third passes; and most touches in the opposition box. Son had scored 7 goals, Maddison had created 26 chances, more than any other EPL player and the team averaged 2.55 competition points per game.

A TICKET TO FLY

Such was the interest in Australia in Postecoglou's progress at Spurs that travel organisations noted a surge in Aussies seeking to travel to the UK on sports holidays. With tickets to Spurs games in short supply, Spurs made an arrangement worth an estimated $A1 million with Ticketblaster to be the club's exclusive ticket-seller in the Aisa-Pacific. The deal was said to guarantee up to 30 "best in house seats", usually reserved for season-ticket holders at Tottenham Hotspur

Stadium. "Having Ange Postecoglou as the coach has really put Australia on the map when it comes to EPL soccer," said Ticketblaster's Rob Davis.

For all the gloom surrounding the results in November-December, Spurs had claimed the scalps of Manchester United and Liverpool, and grabbed draws with defending EPL champion Manchester City and Arsenal – all teams tipped to be prominent at the end of the season.

To be fair, MU was going about its worst start to a season since 1930.

Spurs' effort against Manchester City was particularly noteworthy. The previous season, City won the English Premier League, the FA Cup and the EUFA Champions League. City also went on to win the FIFA Club World Cup in December 2023.

Despite a lack-lustre first half, Spurs managed to recover from a halftime deficit and hold out for a 3-3 draw away at Etihad Stadium.

Spurs finished 2023 with a 3-1 home win in Round 20 over Bournemouth (it was their seventh EPL match in December) still without 10 key players, seven injured and three suspended.

Only two players had played all 20 games – skipper Son and keeper Vicario.

Spurs then were in fifth spot on the EPL ladder, just six

points from leaders Liverpool and one point from the top four.

There was a cost – two more players were injured. If there was an upside, it was that Spurs had only two EPL matches and as it turned out, two FA Cup matches scheduled in January.

There was still much optimism at Tottenham for the second half of the season and beyond. Up to four key players would be returning by February.

Spurs management began work early on their shopping list for key-position players and possible departures in the January transfer window. They had to keep in mind financial regulations and requirements for "home-grown" numbers in the squad.

After 20 rounds the statistics showed the importance of possession. Three of the top five teams enjoyed more than 60% of possession in their matches – Manchester City 63.6, Arsenal 60.3 and Liverpool 60.2. Brighton was the odd-team out, 61.1% of possession but in seventh place. Spurs (5th) and Chelsea (10th) were on 59.2%.

Not being able to finish with a full side on the pitch in a couple of games wasn't helpful to the possession game.

Tottenham Hotspur's run of scoring in each of 32 matches that began in the 2022-23 season was already the longest run in the competition's history. Spurs were the only side to have scored in all of their Premier League games in the first half of the 2023-24 season, including losses.

A FLYING START

With Postecoglou bringing to the club his philosophy on forward pressing, possession control and pin-point passing, Spurs were off to a flyer.

So, what was different about Tottenham Hotspur in 2023-24?

The most obvious point of course was the arrival of Australian Ange Postecoglou.

After just three months, some comparison of statistics began to tell the story and gave fans great hope for the first year of Angeball compared to the 38 rounds of the previous season.

These were some key points:

Passes per match:	Postecoglou 592.20; Conte 474.79.
Pass accuracy:	Postecoglou 88%; Conte 83%.
Goals per match:	Postecoglou 2.20; Conte 1.84.
Big Chances av match:	Postecoglou 2.4; Conte 1.7.
Goals conceded/match:	Postecoglou 0.9; Conte 1.66.
Shots per match av:	Postecoglou 17.8; Conte 13.6.
Shots on target av:	Postecoglou 6.2; Conte 5.2.
Av touches/match:	Postecoglou 755.8; Conte 627.3.
Opp av touches/match:	Postecoglou 515.5; Conte 631.9.

In 2022-23, Antonio Conte's Spurs finished eighth, their worst league season in 14 years. It was 2008 when the last silverware was delivered to Spurs HQ.

Could Postecoglou and Spurs turn things around?

A Top 4 or 5 finish seemed possible, even with several

matches to come. At the least, the club was hoping for a return to European football. Finishing 1 to 4 in the EPL would guarantee them entry into the UEFA Champions League, 5th position would gain entry to the UEFA Europa League if not enough to get them into the Champions League under revised qualification rules. Position 18–20, certainly unlikely, would mean relegation from the EPL.

The team had had 26 competition points from the first quarter of the season, their best start to a top-flight season since 1960-61 when under Bill Nicholson they won their first 11 games and were unbeaten in 16, going on to win the Division One premiership.

The main person keeping a "lid on it" was Postecoglou himself, fully aware that a lot could happen before May 2024.

He talked about building the club's future.

"I don't go into a job not believing I can't make an impact," he said. "That's my role. Like I said a few times, my measure of that is not really having some predetermined timeframe of when that happens… it's just trying to focus on putting the things in place that are important for what we're trying to build.

"We're in a good space… but again we've still got plenty of work to do to make sure what we do now is sustainable. That's the main thing. It's not about making a short-term impact, it's about building something which hopefully brings sustained opportunities of success for the club."

The new "gaffer" at Spurs was celebrated as a breath of "fresh air" around the club and by the media. He was referred to as the "next Alex Ferguson," a tag that would have embarrassed him greatly.

One commentator noted: "The club, the tea ladies, the young players, the other managers, everybody at the club loves him. He's that kind of guy. He's such a fun guy, he's so warm. And then with the media as well, some of the press conferences have been brilliant because he talks about football, but he also talks like if he was your mate at the pub."

The respite from a crowded match schedule, an earlier than expected return of a couple of key players, the resetting of yellow card accumulation after Round 19 and recruitment options promised a slightly happier New Year (2024) for Spurs.

There'd be continuing absences due to injury and international duty, but Spurs still looked likely to be prominent through to the season's end in May.

CHAPTER 4
LIVING THE DREAM

"They're singing his name and they're going to be singing his name for a while. And it's a really, really positive start for Spurs."
Joshua Thomas, Optus Sport.

Tottenham Hotspur sat alone atop the EPL premiership at the start of November 2023, the first time they'd been there since December 2020.

Spurs went two points clear on top of the table by themselves after the October break for international matches, then five points clear for a few days until defending champions Manchester City who had lost two matches found their "mojo" and reduced the lead to two points again,

Nevertheless, the brief five-point lead was Spurs' biggest over a second-placed team in the top-flight since the final day of the 1960-61 season.

Postecoglou set records of his own; he'd won the most points by an EPL manager in their first nine games, 23. The record had been held by another former Socceroos coach, Guus Hiddink, who had 22 points from his first nine games as boss of Norwich in 1992-93.

It was the best start to an EPL season any Spurs manager had ever made and the Spurs' best start to a league campaign since 1960-61, the season they won the League and FA Cup double.

BBC Radio London's Phil Parry: "I'm sure Ange Postecoglou will say 'look, there's still a lot of work to be done', but he's had some backing and he's putting a team together that he wants. He seems to have already worked out what he wants to do, who he wants to do it and how to go about it."

The talking-up of Postecoglou wasn't abating; Arsenal legend Perry Groves (1986-92) and now a media "pundit" in the UK even went as far as to suggest Postecoglou should be considered for the England job.

Postecoglou put that idea to rest in his usual laconic way: "England? Come on mate. They've got a fantastic manager (Gareth Southgate) and I'm eight games into a Tottenham career. That's how I think."

It would be foolish to think other teams wouldn't work out ways to combat Angeball.

As some commentators – and even Postecoglou – noted, there would be "bumps along the way" but fans were enjoying a ride they hadn't been on for some time.

One change about Spurs was significant. While things had not always gone their way early in some games, they still found a way to win. In some of those wins they'd been behind on the scoreboard well into the match. They even managed a 2-1 win over Liverpool with nine men on the pitch at the end.

In games they eventually lost, they'd looked to have winning chances by grabbing early leads.

Star recruit James Madison acknowledged that Postecoglou hadn't been happy with some efforts, even winning ones. "Sometimes we've come off a couple of games where we've actually won and he hasn't been too happy with the performance," he said.

"No manager's ever happy when you're not at your best. He always wants us to play how he wants us to play and that's… non-negotiable."

The significance of press headlines in 2023 was that the word "Angeball" had entered the vernacular, coined during Postecoglou's time in charge of Celtic from 2021.

The key components of Angeball at Celtic: inverted full-backs; building from the back; relentless pressing; creativity of players; retention of possession; limiting opposition possession time.

Search Angeball on the internet: "Angeball is a term used to describe the football philosophy of Angelos (Ange) Postecoglou, the manager of Tottenham Hotspur. It is based on attacking, high-pressing and possession-based football. It has been praised by fans and players for being enjoyable and exciting."

Angeball actually had its origins back in Australia, possibly when a young Postecoglou played for South Melbourne under famed Hungarian manager Ferenc Puskas.

It certainly was evident when he took his first steps on the coaching path in a three-game fill-in gig (all wins) at South Melbourne at the end of the National Premier League's 1996 season. That stint earned him the permanent post.

The immediate effect of Angeball at Tottenham was obvious. The club had its best start in any Premier League season. And the Australian's 26 points and unbeaten run from his opening 10 games in charge was the best return of any new manager in Premier League history.

The previous season under Conte saw Spurs unbeaten after eight rounds, before a collapse ended with them finishing 8th and out of European competition. Conte departed. Postecoglou took over just in time for the start of the new season. Spurs would need to finish at least seventh in the EPL to return to any European competition.

A PLAYER'S PERSPECTIVE

Swedish international Dejan Kulusevski arrived at Spurs on loan from Juventus in the 2022-23 season.

Then 22, Kulusevski played 48 games for Spurs under Conte but told Alasdair Gold, Tottenham Hotspur reporter for *football.london*, he wasn't happy with how his first season panned out for himself and the team, Spurs missing out on European football for the first time in 14 years.

At the end of the season he wasn't even certain of becoming a permanent Spurs player or even whether he would stay there on loan.

The arrival of Postecoglou changed all that, the new manager telling the Swede he wanted him to be part of his plans for Spurs. Kulusevski told a Spurs game-day podcast: "In our first conversation, it was clear we shared the same vision of football. He said he liked me as a player and he thought he could improve me a lot so from the first day it gave me confidence that he wants to use me.

"After that, I listened to his tactics in every game to gain a good understanding of what he wants from me and I'm learning new things every day about the formation. I've had a lot of great coaches but he's a little bit different in every way and it's the first time in my life that I've had a coach like him. He's an unbelievable guy."

Kulusevski proved to be a valuable player as a permanent fixture in the Spurs line-up, on the right wing and in a deeper midfield role. He played in all of the first 17 rounds, averaging 88 minutes on the field and scoring five goals (two assists).

He was enjoying life at Spurs.

"It's so fun. Everybody comes in with a smile on their face because they know they're going to learn new things and we're going to work with the ball to play football. So that's been amazing," he said.

The manager's team talks were always a highlight.

"His team talks have been very good," Kulusevski said. "I like people that speak and are motivational but he's on the top level. He's number one in terms of telling stories and getting us motivated for the games. We learn a lot about life and as players we share a similar outlook on how it should be lived and that you should respect everybody.

"Every time he speaks, it's fun to sit and enjoy whatever he's going to say. He's the sort of coach who makes you want to work hard and it's a pleasure to work with him. I love this mentality because that's how I want to live my life.

"It doesn't matter who you're playing against or what you're doing in life, just go, and if it messes up, it messes up. You did it with your heart. You're not afraid. You're trying to win the game, not trying not to lose the game. I love the game plan.

"I really, really like him a lot. His tactics, his mentality, that's the guy you want to work with. 'No fear, just go!' So I'm really happy to work with him every day, every training session, every game."

Argentinian Giovani Lo Celso who had been out on loan to a Spanish club for 18 months was another player to attribute his turnaround to the arrival of Big Ange, fitting in to an attacking mid-field role with considerable success.

He told Spurs' Match Day program: "In pre-season he told me that he wanted me to stay. I was really grateful for his belief in me, so I worked hard and showed every day that I wanted to be here and play. "I've felt really comfortable in training and in the way he coaches. I love his idea of football which gave me the belief that I could find a place in his team."

CHAPTER 5
REALITY CHECK

There were some sobering statistics for fans as they enthusiastically embraced Angeball.

Postecoglou's record of nine wins, three draws and four defeats with 33 goals scored and 23 goals conceded in the first 16 Premier League games was precisely the same as Antonio Conte's record at that stage of the previous season.

Mid-way through the 2023-24 season (19 rounds), Spurs were in fifth position, just as they were the previous year at the same point, but with one more win to their credit. The rest of the season didn't go well for Spurs and Conte.

The obvious difference from Conte's last year at Spurs was of course Angeball, the style of play that saw Tottenham score a goal in every match to that point, even in a couple of drubbings at the hands of Chelsea and Brighton & Hove Albion.

By Round 22, the difference in Spurs from the previous season had become a little clearer. They were sitting fourth with 43 points from 13 wins, 5 losses and 4 draws (47 goals for, 33 against), when the previous season they were seventh with 39 points from 12 wins, seven losses and three draws

(41 goals for and 31 against). All-out attacks from the deep produced highly entertaining football.

Conte believed in attack from the back, too, but the highball going forward meant possession was too often up for grabs and lost. Postecoglou wanted the ball kept on the ground, and no back-passing.

After his departure from Spurs reports appeared in Italy that Conte had not been happy with the club's transfer activities; the signings of Bentancur and Kulusevski in January 2022, and Richarlison and Bissouma the next summer hadn't paid dividends for him.

Yet, these were the players who figured prominently after Postecoglou took over.

Despite the turnaround from the get-go, the club's lack of depth and key-position players was harshly exposed after just four months. Injury and suspension saw up to 11 members of the first-team squad on the sidelines for some games.

In the first half of the season, van de Ven, Maddison, Solomon, Perisic, Romero, Richarlison, Johnson, Lo Celso, Phillips, Sessegnon, Whiteman (keeper) and Bentancur all spent a month or more on the sidelines. Sarr, Veliz, Udogie and Dier were among players with shorter-term injuries. Several players had hamstring injuries.

All clubs faced injury problems. Spurs, Chelsea and Manchester United were the worst affected, all with 11 players on the EPL "injured list" at the end of 2023.

It was inevitable questions would be asked about Spurs – were the players sufficiently conditioned to sustain Angeball? The EPL injury lists might have suggested no, particularly as Spurs didn't have commitments outside the EPL until the FA Cup rounds in 2024.

Postecoglou: "The way we play takes a fairly hefty physical toll – more than the way other clubs play. For us to sustain and maintain that and be a team, it's no secret we need a strong squad. We're nowhere near that at the moment, understandably so. We're still at the beginning."

Injury numbers don't tell the real story of course. In the case of Spurs, losing key defenders thwarted the Angeball "attack from the back" style.

If Postecoglou was of a mind to pull his hair out in frustration he would have been bald by Christmas as the injuries and suspensions kept coming. Even going into the last game of the calendar year (against Bournemouth), nine players were unavailable due to injury. Two more were injured in that game.

As well, captain Son Heung-min, Yves Bissouma and Pape Matar Sarr were likely absentees for several weeks, on national duty for Asian Cup and Africa Cup of Nations matches (untill their respective teams were eliminated short of reaching the finals in February).

The position looked grim for Spurs' first appearance in the FA Cup in January 2024. Vice-captain Romero and van de Ven made surprise returns in time for the game against Burnley. But 11 players, including Scarlett who had been brought back from loan, were still unavailable until at least the last week of January.

How Postecoglou would have hoped for a magic elixir to get his stars back on the pitch for the New Year!

A crackdown on time wasting which saw up to 12 minutes extra time available in addition to injury stoppages meant games of a regulation 90 minutes sometimes extended to more than 100, with more risk of injury and fatigue.

Postecoglou would have been extremely relieved by Spurs' 1-0 FA Cup victory over Burnley (Spurs entering the competition in the third round) that avoided a replay and an extra game. A last-minute 1-0 loss to Manchester City in the fourth round was disappointing but an upside was there were no further injuries.

Angeball was always going to need strong back-up players, but to put it bluntly, the club's recruitment policies over previous seasons were found sadly wanting when it came to depth.

The recruiting team and Postecoglou had been busy for some months running their eyes over players they would like to have lined up well before the "window" opened. They needed to strike early, something Spurs had not usually done in transfer windows. And strike they did, snaring German Timo Werner on loan from RB Leipzig and Romanian Radu Dragusin from Genoa. Djed Spence was sent to Genoa on loan as part of the Dragusin deal.

Those signings were considered by many as the most significant of the January 2024 trading period.

Postecoglou needed some more talent up front. Son Heung-min became the focal point after the departure of skipper and prolific goal scorer Harry Kane and in his absence with South Korea, Spurs "retrieved" Dane Scarlett, a 19-year-old England Under 21 forward who had been on loan to Ipswich Town in the English Championship.

Asked if he would target young players who could develop, Postecoglou said: "Yeah, because that's what we're trying to build at the moment.

"Guys like Pape Sarr, Destiny (Udogie), Pedro (Porro) and (Dejan) Kulusevski who both (Porro and Kulusevski) became permanent (from loan) they're all in their early 20s, so we're in the first phase of building something. (Sarr re-signed with Spurs in January 2024 for a further six years).

"I think when you've got young guys and you start building something and they grow together, I think it gives you more chance of having sustained success down the road."

Postecoglou saw Spurs as a club that was the preferred destination for players, particularly talented young ones.

"Anyone who's watched us in the first half of the season has seen the aspirations we have to be the kind of football team we want to be," he said.

"We're not the finished product by any stretch, but we're

giving young players an opportunity."

The January 2024 trading period saw almost all EPL clubs send out more players, mostly on loan, than they brought in, probably spooked by the enforcement of financial obligations that saw several clubs in the sights of officials.

In what was an extremely quiet trading period among the usual big-spenders, Draguson was the costliest signing in January 2024, Spurs getting him for €25 million (£21.3 million, $A41.3 million).

FIFA's two-window (northern summer and winter) system was introduced in 2002-03 to restrict players from changing clubs willy-nilly but still allowing them to be traded during set prescribed periods.

Swede Dejan Kulusevski (January 2022) was the best Spurs winter signing of recent times. Could they be just as successful in 2024?

Some players would be leaving. The earliest departure was that of former skipper 37-year-old Frenchman Hugo Loris, who was coming out of contract and joined Los Angeles FC on a free transfer after 11 years at Spurs. Loris wasn't the preferred keeper for 2023-24. Ten other players were sent out on loan, the younger ones to get more regular match experience.

The loss to Brighton just on Christmas meant Spurs had conceded 19 goals since the start of November, equal worst in the EPL with Nottingham Forest.

Spurs picked up just one point from five EPL matches in November and early December.

Despite the dark days of the losses, Postecoglou was philosophical: "I think the important part is... you don't want those periods to come, but when they do come is when I can have the most impact. All eyes are on me; what I do, what decisions I make, how I talk, how I behave. Internally, externally – everyone is looking.

"As much as you don't want to be in these situations, bizarrely I really enjoy it. Because I know what strong beliefs I have in the way I want to do things and now everyone will look and see exactly what I'm all about and what I want from players, staff, people in the club, people outside the club.

"If we can navigate this period like I have done at other clubs it becomes an important foundation and learning tool for what we want to become."

The loss to West Ham on 8 December was the fifth game in succession that Spurs had taken the lead but not won – they lost four of those matches while still attacking hard. A draw had been the best they could do. A victory over Newcastle seemed to put matters right but the subsequent 4-2 loss to Brighton further darkened the mood (it was the first time Spurs had been 2-0 down and trailed by more than a goal at half-time of a Premier League game under Postecoglou).

Discipline became an issue in December, with four red cards dished out. That was the qual highest number (with Liverpool). Bissouma (2), Romero, and Udogie were the recipients. Spurs players also had collected 46 yellow cards at that stage, the third most. Bissouma and Udogie had six each.

Optimism remained. This *Spurs Chat* comment on social media summed up the feelings of many: "Forget about the league table for a second; thank you Ange Postecoglou for changing our football philosophy and the feeling around the club. Thank you for making us Spurs fans count down the days for our next game. Thank you for simply making us enjoy watching Tottenham play football again."

The mood was brighter as Spurs entered the winter break in January 2024 having been unbeaten in five of their most recent six games.

CHAPTER 6
THE REAL DEAL

"The number of times I hear managers saying: 'I would like to play this way but I don't have the players'- I just think: 'Just do it mate...'."

Ange Postecoglou

The headline on *The Telegraph*'s report of the Round 9 victory over Fulham read: "Tottenham are no longer 'Spursy' under Ange Postecoglou – they are the real deal."

"Spursy" was a derogatory chant used by fans after poor showings in previous seasons. It was taken to be a reference to the team's ability for capitulation.

Postecoglou: "If you want to change perceptions, there is only one way to do it. People are not going to change what they think about you because you want them to. You've got to give them a reason to."

Spurs were accused over past seasons of lacking "bottle"; they'd take a lead then blow it. Under Postecoglou they were showing plenty of "bottle" in circumstances that would best be described as chaotic.

Players who showed very little immediately after being

recruited in the Conte era became important in Angeball – Yves Bissouma, Pedro Porro and Destiny Udogie, to name just three.

Chief football correspondent for *The Telegraph* Jason Burt praised Postecoglou for having a "rapidly transformative effect," something he said no other manager had shown in Premier League history.

"The evidence is there. Clear and unequivocal… it remains a relatively small sample size, of course, but Spurs are unrecognisable from the sorry bunch that he inherited," Burt wrote.

"Gone is the negativity, the burden, the sourness…. under Postecoglou, Spurs are the most non-Spursy side possible."

Spurs also regained the respect of other teams, something that had been in decline for decades. Former Manchester United midfielder Roy Keane in his 2014 autobiography, *The Second Half*, mentioned a pre-match MU team talk given by Sir Alex Ferguson before a game with Spurs. "He came in and said: 'Lads, it's Tottenham' and that was it."

In 2023-24 opposing teams were not taking Spurs so lightly.

Many of Postecoglou's changes related to "culture," even simple things such as pre-game preparation.

For home games, for example, the night before a match players and staff were sleeping in their own bed rather than gathering at the training ground and staying in on-site accommodation. They then made their own way to the stadium from home.

Even food menus were changed. Under Conte, *The Evening Standard* noted, ketchup (tomato sauce) and mayonnaise were not permitted in the canteen and players went for long periods eating only plain chicken, salmon and pasta. Ange wasn't quite so dictatorial. The sauce was back.

Postecoglou usually keeps his involvement to match-day preparation and execution. His pre-match address of course is one of the more significant involvements with players.

Captain Son Heung-min: "It's been a fantastic journey for him and for us so far, the way he speaks during his pre-match team talks are incredible. It makes me feel like my heart is bouncing and feel like I want to go out there and give my all for him and this Club, so this has made a huge difference."

The leadership group was new. None of the previous season's leaders were involved as the 2023-24 season began; Harry Kane was no longer at the club and Eric Dier, Hugo Lloris and Pierre-Emile Højbjerg were overlooked.

Postecoglou chose Son Heung-min as the team's new captain, confident he could lead Spurs to the level of success he was seeking. Son had considerable captaincy experience at international level with South Korea, for whom he had 111 caps. Postecoglou had seen him in action when his Socceroos beat South Korea in the 2015 Asian Cup final.

"He has enormous respect among the players," Postecoglou said.

Son: "It's such a big honour to captain this huge club. It was a big surprise and a very proud moment. I've already said to the players that everyone should feel like a captain, on and off the pitch. It's a new season, a fresh start and I will give everything for this shirt and this armband."

The South Korean had scored 145 goals since joining the club in 2015 from Bayern Levenkusen in the Bundesliga, and turned down an offer to move to Saudi Arabia.

While Son was away with South Korea on Asian Cup duty in Qatar in January 2024, he was named as the best Asian player over the past year, for a seventh successive time. He'd scored 27 goals for his club and country in the past 12 months. (A Son goal in extra time for a 2-1 victory put Graham Arnold's Australian Socceroos out of the Asian Cup in their quarter-final match in Qatar in February 2024).

Socialising is not a priority for Postecoglou. He handles the media pretty well. Humility, pragmatism, and being "like a dad," was how one reporter summed up his approach.

There were other changes: staff were being given a schedule for a month at a time, setting out days off and training. There needed to be flexibility of course, even though Spurs didn't have to worry about European fixtures. Team meetings and even training sessions were modified, usually shorter with specific focusses.

Postecoglou's rituals included shaking hands with everyone in the training centre first thing each morning.

The training regime itself was something new. Observers noted a tactical emphasis on low crosses.

Conte had been renowned for punishing pre-season training sessions but sessions under Postecoglou went no longer than 90 minutes, and mostly were ball-oriented. That didn't mean sessions were "easy."

THE FINE MARGINS

Ange on training: "Every day is an excuse to get better. Why do you train? You don't train just to say 'I've trained for a couple of hours' and that's it. You train to try to get better. In any other sport that's how it happens and football is no different as far as I'm concerned.

"If somebody wins the Masters in golf then the next day they're out there on the putting green practising their putting. Why are you practising your putting when you're the best golfer in the world? It's because that's what they have to do because they know fine margins are what make you better.

"Tennis players out there practising their serve or backhand. Footballers are no different. You come in every day and that period when you're out in the field or in the gym, or that period when you're sitting down with your coach going through your video, is an opportunity to improve.

"You're not going to improve a lot (in a single day) but just a little bit. So if you do that every day then that becomes part of who you are. Just walking in, doing your training, getting your bag and going home? No, every day is an opportunity to improve, for me, the players and everyone. So how do I continue to improve a team? By continuously focusing on that."

Spaniard Pedro Porro said there was one constant at training: "There are sessions in which the emphasis is on the defensive part, others on the offensive, but the common denominator is the ball. We always train with the ball. There is a healthy rivalry between team-mates, challenges between each other and an important good feeling to make things work. It wasn't like that before."

Training was geared towards getting players fit enough to play pretty much non-stop. Postecoglou's time at Celtic showed what was expected.

Hamish Carton, a Celtic podcaster and author of *Never Stop: How Ange Postecoglou Brought the Fire Back to Celtic* explained that during training, balls would be thrown back on to the pitch as soon as they stopped rolling. This replicated what happened in matches. Postecoglou's Celtic were extremely quick when it came to restarting play from dead balls such as throw-ins and goal kicks, Carton said.

Carton: "Spurs' ball boys and ball girls will be prominent. It was crazy. There'd be a shot from an opposition player and it would be sailing over and before it would be in the stands Joe Hart would already have kicked off. So many times you'd be at the game and switch off for a moment then look up and Celtic were suddenly at the halfway line already."

Sean Martin, columnist for *TheCelticWay* commented: "It must be exhausting to play against Celtic right now. You spend the majority of the match chasing these blurs of green and white about the pitch, every step wearing you down as it's one more second wasted without getting a kick of the ball. And when you do get it… good luck trying to keep it. They appear like a swarm of green and white bumblebees; buzzing, badgering and bothering until you inevitably can't bat them away or outrun them any longer and it's back to square one again. Pass, pass, pass. Chase, chase, chase."

One thing Spurs players found (and had been warned about) was that they'd be dragged outside their comfort zone.

Ante Milicic, Postecoglou's assistant for almost four years between 2014 and 2017 with the Australia national team: "The players will enjoy his honesty and the way he operates. He'll be very clear about the kind of football he wants to play right from the start. And it'll be immediately obvious to the players that he has something special about him."

ALL IN A DAY'S WORK

A typical working day for Postecoglou?

"I get in early. I'll get up at 6 am, my body clock gets me up at that time so I'll potter around the house for a little bit until the kids get up. Then I'm usually in the training ground at

7.30 am or 8 am every day," he told Alasdair Gold, Tottenham Hotspur correspondent for Football London Online.

"I like my quiet time. That's when I get to think. Once people get in the building then my office invariably gets busy so I get in early just to relax and have a cup of coffee with the quiet to do my thinking for the day. Then I usually stick around until 4.30 pm/5 pm depending on what we're doing in the evening before I get myself home."

Chief football officer Australian Scott Munn also showed a different leadership style. In such a simple exercise as the team photo, he asked for not just players and coaches to be photographed but also of the entire behind-the-scenes staff.

The reality for Spurs on the pitch was there would be defeats. Spurs' entry into the Carabao Cup knockout early in Postecoglou's tenure didn't go well, bowing out to Fulham in a penalty shoot-out. Postecoglou fielded a pretty much experimental line-up to see what he had in the squad.

The 1-0 loss at home in the fourth round of the FA Cup to Manchester City was another missed opportunity to collect silverware (they'd reached the fifth round the previous season). It was the first time Spurs failed to score since March 2023 in their Champions League last-16 second leg match against Milan.

Any chance to collect a trophy was important, as Postecoglou pointed out going into the FA Cup rounds in January 2024.

The FA Cup was "a significant event," Postecoglou said. "Every competition I am in, I want to win. I don't rank them or diminish any against others. The club has history in this. Many of the greatest memories Spurs supporters have will have been in the FA Cup."

If there was an upside to those Cup misses, it was that Spurs could focus all their attention on the second half of the EPL season.

Spurs began the EPL season with a 2-2 away draw with Brentford on Sunday, 13 August 2023. The first win came a week later, 2-0 at home to Manchester United. Spurs remained unbeaten for 10 rounds.

A first loss in the EPL under the new "boss" seemed likely immediately after the competition resumed in September 2023 from the first short break for international matches. Spurs were down 1-0 at home to Sheffield United going into an extended period of extra time. The 12 minutes of stoppage time (arising from the League's crackdown on time-wasting) produced two Spurs goals.

The words that inspired the turnaround? Ones Postecoglou had used before: "We never stop." It was the third time (and not the last) that Spurs came from behind to claim a point or more, and a fourth successive victory – something they didn't manage at all in the previous season.

There was also a touch of EPL history; it was the latest a comeback victory in an EPL match, eclipsing Spurs' own record (95th min v Leicester in January 2022).

There was also a personal milestone for Postecoglou. It was his 50th win in succession coaching a team without losing at "home" – a run that started back in Japan in November 2020 and included 42 victories.

Home games are for the fans, he said, "I do put a big emphasis on that wherever I've been because ultimately for your supporters, as much as you enjoy the away wins because you've got to earn every one of them, it's when they come to their home ground that you want to really reward them."

By the end of October Spurs had won four successive home games. But in November, they lost two home games, to Chelsea and Aston Villa.

A major positive was an away 2-2 draw (coming from behind) against Arsenal in the North London cross-town derby, a real test for Angeball. A 2-1 win over Liverpool followed. At the time of the winter break in January 2024, Liverpool was on top of the ladder and Arsenal fourth.

The Arsenal result created another slice of Spurs history. By taking a point from the draw and despite having trailed twice in the clash, Spurs had earned more premiership points (8) fighting back from losing positions than any other side in Premier League history.

CHAPTER 7
CHANGING THE GAME

Postecoglou spoke often in the early part of the 2023-24 season about what he hoped to bring to Spurs, and how the club's record in the immediate past was not on his mind.

"My reference point isn't what happened the last couple of years, my reference point is where I want the team to be and that is irrespective of where the team has been in recent times.

"When bringing me in the club was aware that things were going to change. Not because of any other reason but because of who I am and the way I do things and the way my teams play.

"I've said before there's no point coming in and tinkering around the edges, we've had to make real changes in everything we did and that's what we've done. Within that context there are some pillars... real basic fundamentals that need to be there and there are a few ways you can emphasise that.

"One is through training and what we do every day and the game gives you those windows of opportunities where if I see something that is not part of what I want us to be as a team then irrespective of the circumstances, whether that is a friendly game, league game, cup game, that's my opportunity to kind of reinforce that to the players."

The way forward was Angeball.

Four decades ago, English football had become so defensive it even found a mention in a parody song ("The Topical Song") by the Barron Nights group in 1979: *"And football's getting so defensive They're playing with eleven goalies."* (trivia note: the group is said to be the only one to tour with both the Beatles and Rolling Stones).

Attack was back in 2023-24.

"I still think our main growth will come in the attacking side of the game," Postecoglou said.

The game was changing, particularly in the way full-backs were used. Few teams used them in the traditional positions as the widest players in a back four. The days of solely two fullbacks were long gone.

Today, the term "inverted fullback" describes the way coaches change the positioning of a full-back when the team has possession to take up a more central position with the midfield.

This was something credited to Pep Guardiola when he was at Bayern Munich in the Bundesliga and now at Manchester City.

Guardiola used former Germany and Bayern Munich fullback Philipp Lahm in this way. Lahm told BBC football writer Raj Chohan that Postecoglou had taken the idea to a "new level" by inverting both his full-backs into the midfield.

Another Spaniard, Arsenal manager Mikel Arteta, also began using one of his fullbacks in a similar role.

Postecoglou's objective was to pull both opposition wingers inside as they tried to press his full-backs, opening the passing lanes to his wingers.

The inverted full-backs also provided his defensive midfielder with short passing options to play through the opposition's second line of pressure. This allowed the team to dominate more possession.

The effect? Spurs began averaging around 60% of possession (ranked fourth in the EPL) compared to 50% (ninth) the previous season under Conte.

At the time of the January 2024 EPL winter break Spurs skipper Son was third on the goal scoring list and Porro third for the most assists from his position at right back/right centre back. The team was averaging 2.14 goals a game while conceding 1.5.

The defenders must be sharp; if possession is lost, they have a lot more ground to cover when needed at the back. This gave rise to questions later in the season on the conditioning of players amid a mounting injury toll. By the 2024 winter break, Spurs had made more tackles than any other side, 428. They were second in goals scored, 44. That's how Angeball works.

Just how good was the possession and passing game of the Spurs? Against Crystal Palace, defender Romero set a then club record for completed passes in a Premier League match, 141 with only one missing its mark. The 11 players of the home side only managed to complete 137 passes between them.

In analysing what was going on inside the Spurs structure, a report by *The Athletic* noted that in the previous season Spurs were allowing opposition teams to make an average 13.8 passes per game before trying to win back the ball. The new season saw that number fall to 10.3.

The Athletic report also identified something else. In the 2-0 win at Bournemouth in Round 3, multiple players covered more than 13 km in the game (typically, an outfielder who plays 90-plus minutes will cover between 10 and 11 kms in a Premier League match, according to data from *SkillCorner*).

The faithful fans who had closely watched the emergence of Angeball noted possession was at the core of the way Spurs played. Overall, there were five identifiable changes.

Higher defensive line: The defenders, especially the centre-backs, operated much further up the pitch, allowing the team to be more dominant in the opposition's half and press further forward.

Inverted fullbacks: Previously, fullbacks (or wingbacks) played wider. Fullbacks were now playing from a more central position, similar to central midfielders. This allowed Spurs to have more players in central areas, leading to better ball control and dominance in the centre.

Wingers positioned higher and wider: The wingers, specifically Son and Kulusevski, played further up the pitch and wider. In the previous system they played more centrally. The change allowed them to stretch the opposition defence and provide width in attack. Son showed his ability and the benefit of the format early in the season with a hat-trick against newly-promoted Burnley in Spurs' 5-2 away victory.

Central midfielders more involved in attack: Bissouma and Maddison were now heavily involved within the attacking third. They collected the ball further forward and created more chances. This allowed Spurs to get more players involved in the final third, leading to better attacking opportunities.

Sweeper-keeper role: The newly recruited goalkeeper, Vicario, played a sweeper keeper role. He was more involved in defence outside the penalty area and would play out from the back, allowing Spurs to control possession and build attacks from deep in their own half.

The Italian Vicario was one of the unsung heroes for Spurs in the first half of the season after he joined the team's goalkeeper squad in 2023.

The statistics show he played in every match to the January winter break in 2024 and had not been subbed off. He'd made 65 saves in 21 EPL games, taken 139 goal kicks and 124 throw-outs. He'd had five clean sheets.

Spurs may have had the lowest goal difference of any top-five team at year's end (scoring 44 and conceding 31) but that was not a reflection on Vicario. If not for his work, many more goals would have been conceded.

He stood firm against some of the best attacking players in the EPL, often behind a defensive line-up that was rarely the same for two weeks in a row due to injuries and suspensions.

The keeper earned high praise from Postecoglou after a 2-1 hard-fought win over Everton on Christmas Eve 2023.

"He has been strong pretty much from the first game," Postecoglou said. "Some games we haven't needed a lot and today we did.

"The saves he made but also the way he dealt with corners was so strong, they put so much pressure on the goalkeeper.

"He's a great shot-stopper and is dealing with a different back four in lots of games. He's got a maturity which helps the team in those moments."

Postecoglou recognised that his greatest challenge would be to alter the "psyche" of players who had been operating under the cautious, counter-attacking styles of past tacticians; that is "re-programming" them to attacking football after nearly four years under Jose Mourinho, Nuno Espirito Santo and Antonio Conte.

Spurs were one of the first clubs to adopt what became known as the passing game, back in the 60s – "play the ball on the floor." A ball in the air could be contested, not controlled.

Conte, who left Spurs "by mutual consent" in March 2023, had complained that there was no chance of changing "the history of Tottenham" any time soon.

"To change this type of situation that has been happening for many, many years in Tottenham, it's not simple," he said. "In a short time it's impossible to do this, not only for me but I think for any manager or coach to come in and change the story in one second. This is the story of this club for the last 20 years."

Some statistics from Postecoglou's time at Celtic in the Scottish League help explain the possession game that is Angeball.

The season before Postecoglou arrived there (2020-21), Celtic scored 78 goals. In his second season (2022-23) they scored 114 – two behind Celtic's all-time record set in 1915-16. In 2020-21 Celtic held possession for an average 66.5% of the time. In 2022-23 that rose to 72.5%, the highest in the league.

It was a case of risk-and-reward; the risk was that turnovers and goals-conceded could increase. The reward though was an historic treble of championship titles included in the five domestic titles he collected of the six available over two seasons.

Postecoglou said in an interview at Celtic: "As much as we get defined by success (winning trophies and winning games) the most pleasing thing for me is the number of goals we've scored. I still think that's the best part of football, it goes beyond winning. Sometimes you can win and not really enjoy a game, but never do you not enjoy a goal. Even the most scrambling, ugliest of goals still gets celebrated. I love the joy goals bring."

The football played by Spurs caught the eye of fans, the pundits and other clubs.

In the Arsenal game in Round 6 a multi-pass move failed to produce a goal, but from goalkeeper Vicario out from his own line, the ball was passed around the pitch 9 times by Spurs players until Porro's cross to the goalmouth at the opposite end was intercepted. Angeball at its best, to quickly get within scoring distance from their own goal-line.

CHAPTER 8
COYS COME ALIVE

Some fans even began to dream of championships as Postecoglou guided Spurs into the top five.

At home games the chants of COYS! COYS! grew louder and more frequent. The chants even went with fans on away games. Come On You Spurs!

Fans also were chanting Postecoglou's name during matches. And "We Love You Tottenham, Yes We Do" was a popular song.

Social media pages of Spurs fans from around the globe – from Africa to Australia and all pitches in between – were brimming with thoughts about Postecoglou and Angeball.

The manager was happy for the fans to be excited. "Let them dream, that's what being a football supporter is all about," Postecoglou said.

"This lot have suffered a fair bit. I'm not going to dampen that. Dreams last as long as they do until somebody wakes you up, so we'll just see," he said.

Fans had long been hungry for EPL success. So was club management. Spurs' best results in the EPL had been runner-up in 2016-17 and third in 2015-16 and again in 2017-18.

The club's most recent trophy was the League Cup in 2008 (Carling Cup, later the Carabao Cup).

The Spurs fans base is one of the biggest in the EPL, even though they share the local populace with north London rivals Arsenal. There is strong support, too in the nearby home counties, Hertfordshire and parts of Essex.

It is thought Spurs may even have more overseas fans than in the UK. There's a really strong fan base in Asia (notably South Korea) and Africa, and fan clubs in many countries including a significant one in Buffalo USA of all places.

All clubs have celebrity fans. Spurs list among their faithful JK Rowling, Adele, Michael McIntyre, Sir Alan Sugar, Mark Wahlberg, Phil Collins, Jude Law, Daniel Craig, Salman Rushdie and "Spiderman" actor Tom Holland. Retired Australian champion swimmer Ian Thorpe is among overseas Spurs fans.

HAPPY DAYS

On the eve of Postecoglou's first game in charge of Spurs against the team he idolised as boy, he was asked how it felt to be facing the Liverpool Reds.

Simply, he said, his days as a Liverpool fan were long gone.

"It was the 70s so you could have gone one or two ways as they only used to show Liverpool or Man United (on Australian TV) back then," he said.

He also spoke of his favourite player of the time. "The

only football they showed [on Australian TV] … was the old English First Division, he said.

"I was a massive Liverpool supporter. Every week, we'd get one or two hours of English football. We'd just take it all in, that would be our buzz for the week. That was the football we grew up on.

"Kenny Dalglish was king for me, I just worshipped everything he did, from Celtic to Liverpool, for Scotland. Then he became manager of Liverpool, so he was the one for me."

Liverpool was his poster team: "Like any kid, I had the posters up on my wall and Liverpool was my team. But you grow up and things change.

"Look, I used to love *Happy Days* (TV show) back then, but I don't have posters of The Fonz on my wall now. It's just the way life is."

As it turned out The Fonz (Henry Winkler, now 77) was watching from afar and was moved to send a message to Postecoglou via a post on X: *"Big Ange, Hello from LA. Congratulations on your win today. Henry Winkler here, AKA The Fonz. ...so if I signed a poster for you right now, would you put it back on your wall? That is the question. Fair dinkum.*

And in response, Spurs sent Fonz his own shirt, signed by Ange with Number 1 on the back. Hopes were high that 2023-24 would bring Happy Days for Spurs.

Ayyyyyyyyye!"

British filmmaker and actor Sir Kenneth Branagh is a Spurs

season-ticket holder. He invited Postecoglou and wife Georgia to a Halloween showing of his production of *King Lear* at London's Wyndham Theatre (Branagh directs and plays the title character).

"Sir Kenneth is a big (lifelong) Spurs fan and was kind enough to invite my wife and I to the theatre," Postecoglou said.

"We don't get too many nights away from the kids, and adult time, so we enjoyed it.

"I did have to swot up on King Lear. It wasn't part of the curriculum at Prahran High where I grew up! I had to do some research.

"You always learn from life and the appreciation of seeing people excel at what they do is inspiring. You walk out of there thinking, 'I don't know how they do it.'

"He (Branagh) was good after it. I caught up with him briefly, he was very kind with his time.

"He was all over how it's going and gave me some little bits of advice, which I'll ignore like he'll ignore my advice on acting, mate!

"It was good. It was much appreciated."

Singer Robbie Williams in 2023 recorded a video remake of his 1997 hit "Angels" with new lyrics honouring Postecoglou, dubbed "Big Ange."

"*And through it all, we're playing the way we want to.*
Big Ange Postecoglou, whether I'm right or wrong.
You can keep your Pochettino, Conte and Mourinho, and

even Christian Gross.

Cause everywhere we go, I'm loving Big Ange instead."

He concluded the video: "I guess I'm a Spurs fan now then." Within a matter of days, the video had recorded more than 85,000 "likes" on social media.

Well before the MU game, shops in the Tottenham High Road were selling outback bush hats, complete with corks, a tribute to their Aussie coach.

Postecoglou was "the man."

CHAPTER 9
COACH OR MANAGER

By the time Burnley and Manchester City faced off across the centre line to open the EPL season on Friday evening 11 August 2023, three of the 20 teams in the competition had new head coaches/managers.

Add to that the number of specialist coaches sacked and there had been 13 managerial departures in the EPL in and immediately after the 2022-23 season, more than in any other season in the league's 31 years. Compare that to the EPL's first season in 1992-93 when just one manager lost his job.

Few football managers survive a career without being sacked. EPL newcomer Ange Postecoglou had been sacked from a club job once, by a third division club in Greece.

Watford – once owned by Elton John and most recently run by Italian businessman Gino Pozzo and family interests – holds the dubious record of having the most sacked managers/coaches, 16 in a decade including 11 while the club was in the EPL. The EPL was established in 1992.

Just three days before the 2023-24 season started, Wolves (Wolverhampston Wanderers) terminated the services of

Julen Lopetegui "by mutual consent". Ex-Bournemouth manager Gary O'Neil took over.

That meant the number of clubs hiring managers since the start of the 2022-23 was 11 out of 20. It didn't take long for another "gaffer" to fall.

Just 14 rounds into the EPL season, Sheffield United showed Paul Heckingbottom the door, the first Premier League manager to be sacked during the 2023-24 season. Round 17 and Nottingham Forest sent Steve Cooper to the unemployment queue. Just 8 rounds later, Roy Hosgson stood down as manager of Crystal Place after 200 games at the helm.

Liverpool manager Jurgen Klopp stunned the football world on 26 January 2024 by announcing that he was stepping down from the job at the end of the season. No doubt he was hoping to bow out of the EPL a winner with The Reds sitting atop the EPL ladder five points clear but with Manchester City pressing.

The German's news got the tongues of the pundits wagging. They were putting two and two together to get six. Wasn't Postecoglou a Reds fan? He'd be a chance to get the job wouldn't he?

Postecoglou said he was as surprised as anyone else by Klopp's decision. "He's a top manager and they (Liverpool) are flying at the moment," he said. "He will go down as one of the best."

Postecoglou was a Liverpool fan growing up. And there's little doubt he dreamed that one day he might be the manager of his favourite team. But he poured cold water on rumours that he was a target for the job.

His history shows he remains loyal to those who take a chance on him. His immediate task – and for the foreseeable future – was to get Spurs on the road to recovery.

As the season progressed, Erik ten Hag came under pressure at Manchester United, as did Roy Hodgson at Crystal Palace. Hodgson, the oldest manager in the EPL, stood down in February after an illness.

Why Spurs for the 57-year-old Australian (he turned 58 in August 2023)?

"I love a challenge," Postecoglou responded when the question was put to him. "I've done that through my whole career. Every step along the way, I've usually moved on the back of success, wherever I've been. It's because there's a challenge out there that really stirs me.

"Firstly, you've got to get asked. That's the first thing; you're not always asked. Secondly you look at what you're going into. The fact that it is – for all intents and purposes – one of the biggest clubs in the world but hasn't had success for a very long time was probably the key driver for me.

"When you go into a challenge like that, you know that should you be able to implement the things you want to, and if it goes well you can make an impact and leave a mark on the club you've worked for. That's what I'm trying to do.

"That was the biggest attraction for me: the fact that the club hasn't had a lot of success, it was coming off the back of a particularly poor season even by its own standards. The opportunity's there to create something."

Interviewed by former player Gary Lineker (*Football Focus*), Postecoglou spoke some more about his objectives: "It can't just be a desperation for a trophy. This club is more than that. I don't see this as a club where just a trophy is enough. I know why there is such a desperation because there's been such a long drought, but it is not what I want to build.

"I want to build a club where every year we are fighting for trophies.

"I have always made decisions against the backdrop I will be here forever, knowing full well I won't be.

"There's always going to be this clock ticking against your tenure and if you let that drive you, you will go mad. I have never seen it work. I have always looked at it thinking 'I will be here for 10 years' and I have never been anywhere more than three years."

It should be noted that a manager and head coach are sometimes interchangeable terms.

When Mauricio Pochettino extended his contract at Tottenham Hotspur in 2016, his job title changed from head coach to manager.

When Ange Postecoglou was appointed in June 2023, the

club's web site mostly referred to him as "head coach" but he was also referred to, particularly in the media, as "manager."

Postecoglou acknowledged his role was coaching, particularly for his first year. After all, he wasn't at the club for the first transfer window of the year (January 2023) and didn't have input in recruiting at the get-go.

Whatever his role in trying to get Spurs back to glory, fans were entitled to ask, who is Ange Postecoglou? He had no English football credentials.

There were doubts, as evidenced by some early social media posts. At one stage there was an aggressive Twitter campaign opposing the Australian's move to Tottenham. In a "'#NOTOPOSTECOGLOU" post, a supporter didn't rate him at all: "deserve better" and "we can't have this guy managing us."

Safe to say Postecoglou's appointment was causing something of a tizz in mainstream media, too. Who was this guy?

All that was, of course, before fans experienced Angeball.

When Spurs started putting points on the board, the fans and the media took notice.

One specialist football web site even dispatched a writer to Melbourne to investigate Ange's early days in South Melbourne and the other places he'd been coaching.

The big Aussie was happy to field questions once he'd settled into his job. He gave in-depth interviews, the most enlightening of them to former Spurs star now-commentator, Gary Lineker.

Lineker, host of *Match of the Day* on the BBC, must have been excited by what he was seeing. Lineker is the only player to have been the top goal-scorer in England with three clubs (Leicester City, Everton and Tottenham Hotspur). He also played for Barcelona in Spain and was capped 80 times for England.

And here was his old side, under the guidance of the relatively unknown Postecoglou, again playing the kind of football in which Lineker himself had excelled (80 goals in 138 appearances for Spurs and 191 goals in a career total of 367 matches).

Postecoglou told Lineker: "I have ended up really late in my career managing one of the most famous clubs in the world in Celtic and one of the biggest football clubs in the world in Tottenham. It has come late, it just took someone to look beyond the norm."

Postecoglou's arrival at Celtic in 2021 wasn't greeted enthusiastically either, despite his record.

At his first press conference in Glasgow he was asked about his credentials for handling the "jump-up" in the level of football he'd entered.

Seemingly a little peeved, but respectful, he responded: "I'm not sure what you mean by jump, but I'm assuming you're saying I worked at a lower level or some lesser level. I guess that's a matter of opinion. I've coached at a World Cup, I've coached against some of the best teams in the world, so that's not how I look at it."

He arrived at Celtic after their disappointing 2020-21 season when they finished 25 points behind the Steven Gerrard-managed Rangers in the 12-team league.

Celtic had competed in the Scottish Premiership, League Cup, Scottish Cup, UEFA Champions League and UEFA Europa League but failed to win a trophy for the first time since 2010.

Postecoglou turned that around, spectacularly.

He completed two seasons at the Celtic Football Club, winning five domestic trophies. His side won 83 of the 113 games in which he was in charge (73.45%).

Joshua Thomas wrote in *The Sporting News* on 12 May 2022: "One of the most surprising managerial appointments in Celtic history has paid off with Ange Postecoglou successfully helping the club reclaim the Scottish Premiership title.

"With first-choice candidate Eddie Howe ultimately turning down Celtic's approaches and later taking the Newcastle United (EPL) job, the Scottish giants decided to take what many viewed as an almighty gamble on a relatively unknown Australian coach.

"A season-opening loss to Hearts had fans even more sceptical, but the Aussie slowly but surely worked his magic to defy the doubters and lead Celtic back to league glory," Thomas wrote.

SHOW AND TELL

Postecoglou took a Celtic team to Sydney in 2022 to contest the inaugural Sydney Super Cup football tournament that also involved Everton and the two Sydney teams, Sydney FC and Western Sydney Wanderers.

Celtic didn't fare all that well, fielding several non-regular first-team players.

But for one young Sydney fan, the highlight involved Postecoglou himself.

Ben dressed as one of his heroes for September Book Week celebrations at his school. He went as Ange Postecoglou, his outfit including a replica Scottish Premiership medal and a copy of Ange's book, *Changing the Game*.

Super Cup organisers spotted a social media post by Ben's dad. They arranged to fly Ben to Sydney on the pretext of taking part in a news item about his Book Week costume and some promotional material for the Sydney Super Cup. Imagine his surprise when Postecoglou was introduced to him in person. Ben interviewed his hero and was probably the happiest of all the fans at the inaugural Sydney Super Cup.

Celtic was so keen to snare Postecoglou that it had to seek dispensation from the Union of European Football

Associations (UEFA) to appoint the Australian who did not at that time have the required European coaching badges. Happily, the club received "recognition and endorsement."

Celtic under Postecoglou may have won two premierships, a Scottish Cup and two League Cups, but there was one disappointment: the performance at Champions League level, against Europe's best, and finishing bottom of their group. Failed shots at goal and turnovers seemed to be the problem (risk and reward not quite in sync).

Nevertheless, his successes at Celtic earned him a nomination in mid-2023 for FIFA Best Men's Coach award for the 2022/23 season. He was named with Pep Guardiola (Manchester City), Simone Inzaghi (Inter Milan), Xavi (Barcelona), and Luciano Spalletti (Italian national team) as candidates.

Postecoglou's FIFA nomination said: "Won a second successive Scottish Premiership title with Celtic FC; won the Scottish Cup and Scottish League Cup to earn the club its eighth domestic treble; named Professional Footballers' Association Scotland Manager of the Season for 2022-23." His work at Spurs was not within the award's timeframe.

Postecoglou understood his success would be measured on the pitch, of course.

"I've always known that, particularly over the last 10 years, every move I've made has come with plenty of question marks around whether I'm up to that level, whatever people perceive that to be," he said as he prepared to get the Spurs season under way. "I've realised the only way I can keep going is to make sure I have success in what I do. The time for reflection will come at the appropriate day."

Wherever Postecoglou had been he was recognised as a football visionary – South Melbourne, the Socceroos, Whittlesea Zebras, Nunawading's junior program, the Victorian Secondary Schools "Elite-V" program, Melbourne Victory, Greece, Brisbane Roar, Japan and Scotland were stopovers on the road to the elite job at N17.

HAVING FUN

Micky van de Ven, Dutch centre-back recruited in 2023, on playing for Ange Postecoglou: "It is so much fun playing football at Tottenham. The assignment is play from the back and if things go wrong, it is the responsibility of the trainer. The manager literally said you can make a mistake. Better that than shooting the ball outside the stadium three times in a row."

CHAPTER 10
INS AND OUTS

Saturday 6 May 1961 is a date that still resonates with older Spurs fans. That was when the club achieved what many felt was impossible at the time, the double of the First Division Championship and Football Association (FA) Cup.

That hadn't been done since Aston Villa in 1896-97. The Spurs attack scored 115 league goals in 1961-62.

How to create a new attacking set-up was something Postecoglou had on his mind almost immediately he took over the reins and set off on his first assignment, a pre-season trip with Spurs to Perth in Western Australia for a "friendly" with West Ham, followed by a trip to South-East Asia for more friendlies.

"Any manager will tell you that part of the key to being a dominant team is having multiple attacking threats and having a midfielder who can score and create goals. They're not easy to come by," Postecoglou said as he headed home to Australia, albeit briefly.

Ange Postecoglou is of course well-known in Australia, particularly in Victoria and its capital, Melbourne.

He spent his playing career with South Melbourne (Hellas)

in the National Soccer League (NSL) from 1984-93. He went on to win premierships with South Melbourne as a player, then as coach.

He had also represented Australia as a player, coached club sides in the national league and eventually became head coach of the national side until he resigned and took a club position in Japan. He was inducted into the Football Australia Hall of Fame in 2022.

The job at Spurs was something of a hot-seat given the penchant of chairman Daniel Levy (the longest serving chairman in the EPL) for making changes at the top when success wasn't forthcoming. The club's most recent trophy was in 2008 and since 2001 when Levy became chairman the club had appointed 12 managers, Postecoglou the latest.

Spurs, majority-owned by ENIC International Ltd, were in turmoil towards the end of the 2022-23 season. They'd finished fourth the previous season.

On 26 March head coach Antonio Conte left "by mutual agreement." He was replaced immediately by Cristian Stellini, appointed acting head coach for the rest of the season that was to end on 28 May.

But on 24 April after a 6-1 loss to Newcastle United, Stellini was sacked and replaced by Ryan Mason as interim head coach until the end of the season.

It was Mason's second stint as fill-in boss at Spurs. A former Spurs player, Mason previously was appointed head coach at

Spurs until the end of the 2021-22 season after Jose Mourinho was sacked in April 2021. The Portuguese manager didn't take his dismissal kindly. "I hope the Tottenham fans don't get me wrong but the only club in my career where I still don't have a deep feeling for is Tottenham," he said. Two and a half years later, he was shown the door by Italian Serie A club Roma, despite having won a UEFA Europa Conference League trophy in the 2021-22 season.

As Spurs parted company with Jose Mourinho in 2021 after 17 months in charge, and installed Nuna Espirito Santo, Ange Postecoglou was up north, starting a run at an historic treble of domestic trophies – the Scottish Premiership, the League Premiership and the Scottish FA Cup.

By any measure, 2023 was a good year, Postecoglou capping off what he'd started in 2021-22.

Celtic were keen to keep him on board.

But the Australian always harboured a desire to coach at the top level in Europe and that meant the EPL.

He was represented by Australian "super agent" Frank Trimboli. London-based sports agent Trimboli had brokered some of the biggest transfers in the main European leagues, particularly in England, Italy and Spain.

Trimboli co-founded Base Soccer with Leon Angel. The company was acquired by CAA Sports in July 2019, becoming CAA Base.

The Perth-raised Trimboli had represented Postecoglou

for several years. According to London reports, he also was a longtime confidant of Spurs chairman Levy; probably the link between Postecoglou and a move to Spurs. He also represented key Spurs players Son Heung-min and James Maddison.

Trimboli was reported to have visited Celtic a couple of weeks before Postecoglou was announced in June 2023 as the new "gaffer" at Spurs on a four-year deal.

Spurs fans were hoping Postecoglou and his penchant for attacking football was the right person to achieve premiership glory the club hadn't experienced since 1961 (First Division) under Bill Nicholson.

The club's last trophy came in the League Cup in 2008 under Spaniard Juande Ramos, hardly a satisfactory record for one of the biggest clubs in England and one of the Premier League's "Big Six".

Esteemed managers including Harry Redknapp, Mauricio Pochettino and Jose Mourinho all tried to bring silverware home to North London and failed.

Postecoglou's father Jim (Dimitris) died in 2018. Ange knew what advice his father would have given him: "Don't stuff it up, mate."

Spurs assembled a coaching staff around Postecoglou; Postecoglou rarely took his own staff with him when he changed jobs. At Spurs, there was least one familiar face (to Australians, and Postecoglou) among the troops, former Socceroo Mile Jedinak. He said of his role: "Part of the responsibility is working with individuals and units with an emphasis on set-plays, and defensively as well, that is something I have responsibility for which I'm enjoying also."

Jedinak, 39, became national captain under coach Postecoglou in 2014 and led the Socceroos through two FIFA World Cup campaigns, in Brazil and Russia.

He'd also played for Crystal Palace and Aston Villa in England as a defensive mid-fielder.

Jedinak was appointed assistant coach at Spurs in 2023 after working as a youth coach and loan-development coach at Villa.

At Celtic, Postecoglou had another former Socceroo star Harry Kewell as an assistant (First Team) coach in 2022.

Ante Milicic, Postecoglou's one-time assistant with the Socceroos, saw Jedinak's arrival at Spurs as highly significant.

"Such a great professional, and a great attitude," Milicic said. "Like Ange, he had quite a winding road to get to where he is. He was an excellent captain and presence in the dressing room. He'll be a good buffer for Ange at Tottenham and is one of the best that I've ever worked with. I'm really excited to see how he gets on there — it's such a smart appointment.

"And it's a great opportunity for Mile. Working with Ange is like getting a PhD in coaching — after working with him I felt like I could do any job.

"Ange believes in Aussie coaches and players and breaking down barriers, and he will help those that want to be helped. But he's very smart and selective, he won't just help anyone."

Others on the Spurs coaching staff were Chris Davies (new) and Rob Burch (returning), who joined Ryan Mason and Matt Wells.

Spurs recruited another Australian. Scott Munn was employed as Tottenham's new chief football officer from September 2023. His start was delayed by the completion of contractual arrangements at his previous job.

Munn previously held executive roles in Australia's AFL (including the establishment of a team on the Gold Coast in Queensland), NRL, football (soccer) and the Sydney Olympics organisation. He had been chief executive of Melbourne City FC in Australia's A-League from 2009 (when it was Melbourne Heart) before moving to China to head the City Football Group's operations there for four years until recruited by Tottenham. He was taking charge of all Spurs footballing departments.

In October 2023, Spurs named former global director of football development and international academies at Aston Villa, Johan Lange (originally from Denmark), as the club's new technical director. He was to "have responsibility for recruitment, analytics and talent identification" across senior and academy teams. He previously worked at FC Copenhagen as assistant manager as well as development director and technical director.

Rob Mackenzie, who had previously worked at Tottenham, followed Lange from Aston Villa to Tottenham to become the club's new chief scout.

With Lange came Frederik Leth, the head of football research.

Spurs saw these appointments as vital in getting ready for the 2024 and later transfer windows.

"It is important they come in now. The January window, like for every club, is an important one. My view on the January one is that if you can get your business done early in the window it certainly is more helpful because you leave it until the end of January and sometimes what you try to gain you've missed that opportunity by waiting a whole month," Postecoglou said.

The task for Lange's team would be to identify talent that might suit Postecoglou's plans. He would have already identified (and itemised) what kind of players he wanted. The recruiters would then have to provide him with a list of prospects.

A manager and coaching team may have been settled and the competition well under way, but Postecoglou still had challenges.

At Celtic, it took less than a year for Postecoglou to put to rest any doubts about what he could achieve. He revitalised a club in turmoil, winning the Premiership title and League Cup in his debut season. And followed that up with even more success the next.

Spurs were looking for a similar degree of success. Was Postecoglou their Messiah?

CHAPTER 11
THE MONEY MARKET

Postecoglou's salary at Spurs wasn't immediately disclosed but it was reported he was on £2.2 million (about $A4.2 million) at Celtic for 2022-23. Spurs reportedly paid just under £5 million ($A9.7 million) in compensation to Celtic when they lured the Australian to North London.

Pep Guardiola at Manchester City is one of the highest-paid football managers in the world and the highest-paid in the EPL, on a salary of £20 million ($A39 million), according to press reports . The next highest-paid managers were Jurgen Klopp at Liverpool (£15 million, $A29 million), Erik ten Hag at Manchester United (£9 million, $A17.5 million), Mikel Arteta at Arsenal (£8.3 million, $A16.2 million), and David Moyes at West Ham (£5 million, $A9.7 million).

It could be assumed that Postecoglou's starting salary would be around £5 million, as Tottenham is one of the "Big Six" teams in the EPL.

Not a bad earner for someone who as a five-year-old fled his native Greece with his family that had nothing but a couple of suitcases containing their belongings when they disembarked in Melbourne, Australia, in 1970.

From those days forward it was pretty much an upwards spiral for Postecoglou, albeit with some hiccups. As a player, he captained his club side and represented Australia. But he always knew he'd be coaching.

He went on to coach the Australian national team (the Socceroos) but acknowledged he preferred the challenges of club football. For one thing, games involving national teams weren't all that frequent for Australia, and dealing with national associations could often be quite prickly.

He was also disappointed the achievements of the Socceroos didn't get the recognition they should have.

Even the shock 3-1 win by Frank Farina's Socceroos over England in 2003, in England to boot, had become a distant memory. The home team boasted Beckham, Lampard, Scholes, Ferdinand, Owen and Rooney but the upset didn't provide the boost to the code in Australia that it should have.

Perhaps not enough significance is attached to international "friendlies" even though the world's best players are involved.

Postecoglou coached the Socceroos when they lost 2-1 to England at Sunderland in 2016, a creditable effort by any standard, but one that also went virtually unheralded, as did the Graham Arnold-managed team's 1-0 loss to the home team in England in October 2023. Arnold was Farina's assistant in 2003.

Postecoglou said: "Unfortunately from my days as national

coach we were going backwards in terms of we don't see it as an investment, we see it as an expense. We just have too (much) short-term thinking, there just aren't enough people with a broader vision as to how we can actually make Australia a force in world football."

Perhaps his arrival at Tottenham and the outstanding achievement by Australia's Matildas in reaching the semi-finals of the 2023 women's World Cup would be a big step in rectifying that situation.

But Postecoglou wasn't sure there'd be a lasting legacy from the effort by the Matildas.

"When you look at what the Matildas did at the World Cup, unbelievable, but you still won't see an influx of resources to the game. You won't. I guarantee it," he said. "They'll build stadiums and other codes will use them.

"I just don't think the nation as a whole has that inside them to understand you can make an impact on the world of football, but it requires a kind of nationalistic approach that I just don't think Australians at their core are really interested in."

At Spurs, Postecoglou would be managing a team list that was worth, according to *transfermarket.com*, more than €760 million (£650 million, $A1,300 million).

Teams in the EPL had a combined market value of €0.42 billion (about $A700 billion), more than half of the teams were worth more than €352 million ($A574 million).

THE MONEY MARKET

According to a UEFA report, Manchester United's squad at the end of the 2023 financial year had cost £1.2 billion ($A2.33 billion), the most expensive squad ever assembled in Europe and supassing the previous record of Real Madrid's £1.13 billion ($A2.18 billion) in 2020.

The 20 EPL teams (with promotion and relegation each year) are permitted 25 players in their squads, eight of whom had to be "home-grown" and no more than 17 "non-home-grown." Clubs also field women's teams, Under-21s and Under-18s. Squads must be finalised in mid-September for the first part of each season through to the month-long transfer "window" in January. Under-21 players are eligible over and above the limit of 25 players per squad.

In the EPL, as in many other team sports, success on the pitch (trophies) is the only acceptable outcome.

It is a cruel fact of professional sporting life that if a team worth millions of dollars (or pounds, or euros) is not performing, replacing a much less expensive manager is the usual way of dealing with the situation.

Paying out an expensive player's contract inhibits the ability to recruit a similarly expensive replacement – such action is rare, even if not unknown. If a high-priced player is sacked it will more likely be for disciplinary reasons. Trades, though, are a regular occurrence. Players also can be sent on loan to another club either at home or abroad, particularly useful in allowing emerging players to gain match-time experience rather than warming a bench. Loans can also include options to buy.

It must be noted to those unfamiliar with the system, that the massive amounts of money bandied about in transfer talk are not the amounts paid to the player. A transfer fee is the amount paid by one club to another to acquire a professional footballer's contract (playing services). A player's salary is a separate figure but, in most cases, players receive a percentage of the transfer fee they generate.

For example, Tottenham Hotspur paid £60 million ($A117 million) to Everton for Richarlison in 2022 – his base salary was put at £90,000 ($A175,000) per week.

The EPL's two transfer "windows" (winter and summer) generally coincide with those across Europe.

Transfer negotiations can be complex, but the principle seems to be "bid low and go high" to seal a deal. Through all the haggling, most fans only are interested in the final lineup.

According to Deloitte, £255 million ($A497 million) was spent on the last day of the (northern) summer transfer window in September 2023.

Tottenham Hotspur made the second biggest deal on the final day, snaring Brennan Johnson from Nottingham Forest for £45.5 million ($A88.7 million). The biggest signing was Manchester City's deal to get Portugal midfielder Matheus Nunes from Wolves for £55 million ($A107 million).

According to data from *spotrac.com*, Manchester City

already had the three highest paid players in the EPL: Kevin de Bruyne on £400,000 ($A780,000) a week, Erling Haaland on £375,000 ($A730,000) a week and Jadon Sancho on £350,000 ($A682,000) a week. Contract earnings were supplemented by add-ons such as endorsements and individual sponsorships. The two Manchester clubs had 14 of the top 25 highest earners in the League.

Chelsea was the biggest spending club, laying out close to £1.0 billion ($A1.9 billion) to sign key players, partly offset by nine sales.

According to *Transfermarkt.com*, the top 10 most valuable EPL teams for the first half of the 2023-24 season, as distinct from the 2023 financial year, after the summer transfer window, were:

1. Manchester City £1.01 billion ($A1.9 billion);
2. Arsenal £950 million;
3. Chelsea £790 million;
4. Manchester United £758 million;
5. Liverpool £707 million;
6. Tottenham £620 million;
7. Aston Villa £519 million;
8. Newcastle £514 million;
9. West Ham £376 million;
10. Nottingham Forest £342 million.

Spurs spent more than £150 million ($A288 million) in the second transfer window of 2023 on nine new signings and lost England captain Harry Kane to Bayern Munich (for $A169 million).

Arrivals were Brennan Johnson (£47.5 million, Nottingham Forest); Ashley Phillips (£2 million, Blackburn Rovers); Manor Solomon (free transfer, Shakhtar Donetsk); Guglielmo Vicario (£16.3 million, Empoli); James Maddison (£40 million, Leicester City); Pedro Porro (£34 million, Sporting CP); Dejan Kulusevski (£25.6 million, Juventus); Micky van de Ven (£34.5 million, Wolfsburg) and Alejo Véliz (£13 million, Rosario Central). Kane and 14 other players were moved on.

A strict enforcement of EPL profit and sustainability rules (PSR) saw Everton losing 10 competition points for breaches in 2023, dropping them down dangerously close to the relegation zone. An appeal reduced the points loss to 6.

The "money police" weren't done. Everton (again), Nottingham Forest, Chelsea and Manchester City were among the clubs either charged or investigated for their spending going into 2024. Non-compliance could incur monetary penalties as well as loss of points.

PSR allows clubs to lose £105 million ($A203 million) over three seasons, or £35 million ($A68 million) a season, on a rolling basis on the proviso that £90 million ($A174 million) is covered by secure funding from owners, such as buying more shares instead of giving their clubs a loan. The three-year losses allowed without such guarantees are £15 million

($A29 million).

Scrutiny of finances under PSR meant clubs had to be vigilant about their spending during the two annual trade windows.

While clubs in the UK are familiar with approaches from other European clubs, the summer window of 2023 saw Saudi clubs, bankrolled by the $US620 billion Public Investment Fund (PIF), enter the player market.

The three highest-paid players in world football were playing in the Saudi Pro League. Neymar was on £240 million ($A468 million) a year at Al Hilal, Ronaldo was on £173 million ($A337 million) a year at Al Nassr and Benzam was on £172 million ($A335 million) a year at Al-Ittihad. All three clubs are owned by the PIF.

PIF already was funding major golf (including the breakaway LIV series), Formula 1, cycling, WWE, boxing and several other significant sporting organisations and events. The sovereign wealth fund was established in 1971 to reduce Saudi Arabia's economic dependence on oil by diversifying its investments and generating profits across a variety of sectors.

Players are not PIF's only interest in English football. In 2021, PIF took an 80% stake in EPL team Newcastle United.

Coaches, too, were on the Saudi Shopping list. Former Liverpool captain Steven Gerrard, sacked as manager by Aston Villa in 2022, joined the Al Ettifaq club in 2023.

CHAPTER 12
OUT OF ATHENS

On the morning of 21 April 1967, Greeks in Athens awoke to the rumble of tanks, occasional rifle shots, and military songs playing on the radio.

A radio announcement said: "The Hellenic Armed Forces have undertaken the governance of the country."

Colonel Georgios Papadopoulos, Brigadier General Stylianos Pattakos and Colonel Nikolaos Makarezos ordered the tanks to roll into Athens.

The reason for the coup given by the military junta was that Greece was in danger of falling into communist rule.

The overthrow of the caretaker government came a month before scheduled elections that Georgios Papandreou's Centre Union was favored to win.

During the night of the coup, 16,000 people – mainly members of the Parliament, journalists, labour leaders, and members of left-wing organisations – were rounded up. Some were jailed, others kept under house arrest or sent to the Yaros Island concentration camp. Torture and killings were reported.

Resistance against the colonels within Greece and from

abroad lasted for the seven years of their rule.

Human rights violations were rife. Criticism of the junta, including accusations of theft from businesses, was met with imprisonment.

The right-wing military junta that seized control in 1967, referred to as the Regime of the Colonels, ruled Greece from 1967 to 1974.

In 1973 the monarchy was abolished.

To briefly summarise a complex series of events, the junta fell on 24 July 1974 in another coup, led by hardliner Dimitrios Ioannidis, head of the military police. His rule collapsed quickly.

The five days between July 20 and 24, 1974, were the most turbulent, and the most decisive, in modern Greek history. The Turkish invasion of Cyprus, the collapse of the military junta, and the birth of the new Hellenic Republic, all happened in that period.

Constantine Karamanlis, once self-exiled to Paris, returned on 24 July 1974 and formed a government of national unity to lead recovery from the seven-year military rule.

On 8 December, in a referendum about the establishment of a Republic or the return of exiled King Constantine II, 69.2% of Greeks decided on a Republic over a return of the monarchy. The modern Hellenic Republic, as it is known today, was established.

What happened in Greece back in 1967 was something

Greeks, including the many living in Australia, wanted to consign to history. Melbourne was said to have the largest Greek population outside Greece. At the 2021 census, 92,314 Australian residents were born in Greece, 424,750 people said they had Greek ancestry (either alone or in combination with another ancestry), comprising 1.7% of the Australian population.

At the time of the 1967 coup, Dimitris Postecoglou operated a business in Athens.

He and wife Voula had a young family. Son Angelos was just two years old. (born on 27 August 1965). Daughter Liz was seven. They lived in the Athens suburb of Nea Filadelfeia.

Three years later, Dimitris's business, cabinet-making, had been lost under military rule. The family – Dimitris, Voula and their two children – were on the Chandris Line ship *Patris* heading to Australia, their belongings in a couple of suitcases.

Patris made 91 voyages to Australia between 1959 and 1975 taking tens of thousands of Greek migrants (and other nationalities) to Australia. The *Patris* travelled regularly via Egypt's Suez Canal. When the Suez closed in 1967, the ship spent the next five years detouring around Africa, the route the Postecoglous were on. The journey took a month.

"Patris" is the Greek word for 'homeland'. The ship's first port of call usually was Fremantle in Western Australia, then Melbourne, carrying 1,076 passengers in single-class accommodation.

The ship's former vice-captain Nikolaus Soutos told SBS Television that those who travelled to Australia aboard *Patris* felt a powerful connection to the ship, "because no one knew where they were travelling to – they were to be thousands of miles away from their families, (who didn't know) if he or she would come back home ever again."

The passengers were in a tough position psychologically, he said, because they were going to a country with a different culture totally foreign to them.

Many people were uneducated, not knowing anything of the English language and the majority did not have any professional skills.

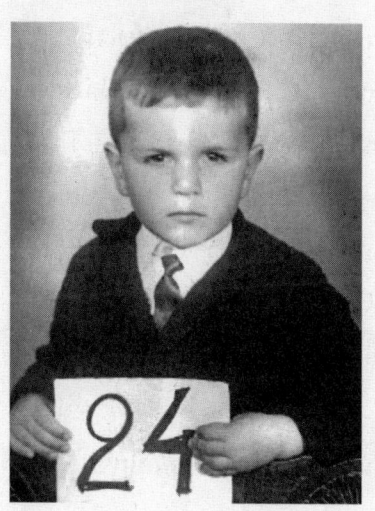

Ange Postecoglou was only five. When he disembarked in Melbourne, he carried a sign with number 24, his personal passenger number on his family's voyage.

That steely look became something of a trademark even into in his coaching years.

Tim Cahill said the young boy was looking at the camera in the same way he would years later, as coach of the Australian team, regularly "burning a hole in the back of his players' heads" at training.

Friend and teammate Paul Trimboli said Postecoglou didn't talk much and he didn't make people feel comfortable and "it could be unsettling" for a lot of people.

Postecoglou spoke a bit more about going to Australia in an interview with Gary Linker after arriving at Spurs in 2023.

"We were immigrants," he said. "I don't look like your typical refugee, but I was five years old when we came, we went by boat, and had no certainty about anything.

"At the time Australia was looking towards immigrants to help with the workforce, my dad was an unskilled labourer, so we took that leap, stayed in a refugee camp for a while, then got a house." The family settled in the suburb of Prahran.

Postecoglou was amazed at what his parents did.

"What they would have gone through to take a young family halfway round the world, on a ship that takes us 30 days, to a country where they don't speak the language, they don't know a soul, they don't have a house, they don't have jobs," he said.

"I don't have great recollections of it. At the time, there was a bit of upheaval in Greece and, unfortunately, we got caught up with that.

"My father made the decision that we needed to move abroad.

"People say they go to another country for a better life. My parents did not have a better life; they went to Australia to provide opportunities for me to have a better life."

Postecoglou said later he had learned plenty of life lessons from seeing what his mother and father went through as they settled in a new country.

"I can't remember it being hard, but now as an adult, as a parent, I look back and realise just how tough it was, particularly for my parents," he said. "We went to Australia, we had no family, no friends, we were literally refugees."

In a *Skysports.com* interview in 2022 he said: "I was very aware that we were different. My father, my mother, they literally had to make their way around without being able to talk (in English). That leaves you, I guess, very isolated in many respects.

"There is the story of my dad being alerted by a neighbour that there was a mattress out the front of a house for whoever wanted it. They picked it up (in the dark) and were lugging it on their shoulders but forgot where home was and were literally walking the streets for hours because they could not even ask for directions.

"My dad used to tell that story and get a lot of laughs but I am sure when he was lugging that mattress on his shoulders it was not funny.

"I have a feeling he thought he would go to another country, establish ourselves, and he could get his family into a situation whereby they would be comfortable enough for us to go back and live our lives in Greece.

"There was a never-ending struggle to establish ourselves. He was working day and night, my mum was working, we were at school, we were saving money to buy a house. We shared a house with another family for a number of years.

"All those kinds of things sort of cascade and in the end his life just sort of revolved around working and trying to make a living for us to survive rather than thrive pretty quickly."

Once settled, Ange's parents legally changed the family name to Postekos. His father went by an anglicised version of his name, "Jim".

Ange didn't really think much about his name until he was picked in an Australian youth team as an 18-year-old. "When it came to my first passport, and my first driver's licence, there was nothing I could do about it," he said.

It appears Postekos may still be his registered name. A company called "Big Ange Limited" was incorporated on 23 October 2023 with one active director, listed as Angelos Postekos ("Australian, Director, Football Manager, Born in Aug 1965") with its HQ at Queen Victoria Street London.

Ange's parents gained citizenship in 1977 under the name of Postekos. His sister took citizenship two years later. They lived in the Melbourne suburb of Windsor, next door to Prahran where many Greek migrants settled. People of Greek heritage are now spread far and wide throughout greater Melbourne, the suburb of Oakleigh being a main hub. Lonsdale Street in the CBD has been the centre of Greek cultural activity, such as the annual Antipodes Festival that has been held for more than 30 years.

Several soccer clubs were formed by Greek communities, the most famous being South Melbourne Hellas and Heidelberg Alexander. Greek immigrants contributed to all facets of Melbourne's cultural and social life, politics at federal, State and local government levels, and sport, particularly soccer.

Ange's sister Liz told an interviewer: "Early days were a bit tough because of the name (Postecoglou).

"Mum and Dad changed it to make our life easier for us, because as a kid it's very difficult to have to spell your name letter by letter.

"It was shortened from Postecoglou to Postekos. But from a very young age he (Ange) was beloved in the Greek press and Peter Desira (soccer reporter) formed a bond with Ange.

"The media had got used to the Postecoglou name and it stuck, despite Postekos still being on his passport. So legally he was Postekos but in the media he was Postecoglou.

"He's a bit of a traditionalist, so he's proud of that name. He never changed it in the media and he could have."

Ange remained proud of his background but happily became an Australian citizen. The name Postekos remained on youth team sheets until he started using his original surname.

Growing up wasn't easy. "As a kid I just wanted to fit in and the best way to fit in was sport," he once said.

That sport was football – or soccer as it was more widely known in Australia.

There was one particular thing a lot of migrants from Europe brought with them – the round football.

As Mike Petersen, a friend and former South Melbourne player, recalled, "it wasn't cool to play soccer when Ange and I were growing up. It was called either kiss chasey or wogball. Kiss chasey because after the boys scored a goal everyone would be hugging and kissing and wogball because only the ethnics played it," he said.

Most of Ange's most memorable times as a child were to do with football.

He conceded his father was not the "warm and cuddly" type, but football was their common bond.

"My dad first took me down to South Melbourne when I was eight and I joined the club when I was nine. Those are the strongest memories of my youth. It was a big part of my childhood," he recalled.

"For us, Middle Park (football ground) became almost the social hub for Greek-Australian migrants. It almost became our church and it is significant that it was a Sunday because it was a place where we found community.

"It was a unique atmosphere, a sense of community, a passionate vocal crowd, and it made a strong impression on me as a young kid."

As an 8-year-old (going on 9) he watched on a black and white television set (colour wasn't widely available until 1975) as Australia made its first appearance in the World Cup finals, in 1974. Thirty-nine years later he was appointed coach of the Australian Socceroos and set them on the road to World Cup play-offs again.

When he joined South Melbourne Hellas as a nine-year-old an incredible journey began.

The family had settled in the heart of Hellas territory.

He recalled: "I was obsessed with the game somewhere deep inside me even as a young boy. I kind of knew that whatever journey I was on, football was going to be at the middle of it."

Coaching became his "thing," compiling an impressive story over several years.

It is fair to say he found breaking into coaching in Europe had almost become a dream too far.

He had interviews that mostly drew blank faces.

While he'd hoped for "a flicker of recognition there about something" he said he didn't seem to be seriously recognised as a candidate.

"But that's OK, that's just my journey," he said. "I don't say that for people to kind of think 'woe is me'. I love my journey. It's made me the man I am today. I've had unbelievable experiences. There's always different ways to get to the highest level.

"I didn't think I would (make it), but if I didn't it wouldn't have diminished my life and my career. I still would have felt like I had achieved all I had wanted because I've made an impact wherever I've been. That's the only thing you can control. From that perspective, it's just part of my journey. Other people have different ones."

It is doubtful if many – or even any – top-flight managers or coaches started out on a journey to the top in the same way as Ange Postecoglou.

CHAPTER 13
KID'S STUFF

The early years for the Postecoglou family in Melbourne, Australia, were not that easy.

Ange's sister, Liz, is five years older and recalled the early time in Melbourne for the documentary *The Age of Ange* for the ABC's *Australian Story* series in 2015.

"They (parents) arrived here with just suitcases, having to care for two little children," she said. "It was difficult for her (Voula, her mother). I remember many nights hearing her crying."

Postecoglou's father – Dimitris (sometimes Dimitrios), better known as Jim – was a hard worker. Up early, home late. Football was his escape.

"The only time I ever got to see any joy in my dad was when we went to the football on a Sunday," Postecoglou once said. "So that made an impression on me because I made a quick connection that football makes him happy… so if I love this like he does, it will get me close to him."

Looking back on those years, he told Hamish McLachlan in a 2017 interview for Melbourne's *Herald Sun* newspaper:

"What I cherished the most was the two-hour window on a Sunday where we used to walk through the Middle Park gates at the old South Melbourne Hellas, and he would become a different bloke. Passionate, sociable, talkative, he just loved it. I remember looking up at him when I was about six or seven and thinking 'That's what I want'. Those Sundays are my most treasured memories."

Angelos settled in quite quickly. He didn't experience terrible racial taunts and felt relatively at home in his new life, kicking a soccer ball around in the streets with the other kids, mostly his mates from Prahran State School.

The family's living arrangements were sometimes challenging.

"Sharing a house with other families was tough at times and you didn't have a lot of private space," he said.

"But I never felt I was wanting for anything."

He acknowledged that his parents did all they could to give their children a better life. He has often spoken of his admiration for their efforts.

For an Hellenic Museum project in 2012 he said: "I reckon it was a pretty tough life for my parents. There were some dark periods for them. My dad's got a great sense of humour and I always remember that when he was in a good mood it was fantastic; as well I also remember he sometimes really struggled with things, and my mum struggled with things, too.

"I pretty much remember having a fairly happy childhood.

I don't think there were too many issues growing up. I remember my dad and my mum working really hard.

"I had a five-year (age) difference with my sister and we were never in school at the same school, state or high school, so I guess growing up mainly through sport is how I made my connections. I spent much of my childhood being outdoors."

Being Greek didn't seem to trouble him much, except for having to regularly spell his surname to teachers and classmates, a problem recognised early by his father. Postekos was much easier to pronounce, and spell.

"As a kid, I just wanted to fit in. I didn't necessarily like the fact I came from another country and had a really long surname that nobody could get their mouth around. For a young boy the best way to fit in was sport," Postecoglou recalled.

SANDWICHED

"You'd go to school and everybody would open their packed lunches. So everybody had their Vegemite sandwiches. And I'd open mine up and you'd get cheese, salami, olives and taramasalata... and they were all like: 'What the hell is going on?'"

Ange was mad about sport by that time. It fitted in well with his father's love of football. He recalled how his father used to wake him up at night to watch games being televised from the UK. He became a Liverpool fan.

Soccer was a passion: "I remember being nine or ten years old and buying the newspaper every morning just to read the soccer. I usually got 20 cents for lunch money and I'd spend five cents on the newspaper, just to read the soccer results and what was going on in the world."

His sister Liz recalled in the *Australian Story* documentary: "He was like a sponge. Anything to do with soccer he absorbed. He would sit in on conversations among older people as they discussed it. He would watch what little television there was in those days. Magazines, books, stories, anything."

Postecoglou spoke of his infatuation with coaching as a youngster: "I always wanted to be a manager," he told commentator Gary Lineker in 2023. "I loved the game. I loved all of it, not just playing. I would get three-month-old Shoot magazines, Roy of the Rovers. I would read everything. I was a massive Liverpool fan, I loved Bill Shankly, I loved the boot room stories."

Ange Postecoglou went on to Prahran High School. Imagine his reaction – and that of his mates, too – when they found there was no soccer program. No soccer, but Angelos Postekos wasn't deterred from playing some kind of football; he took on the Australian game.

He recalled the season he played Australian Rules football at school, the only football available.

"Like all kids, I wanted to fit in," he said. "And because I was pretty athletic, I found that I was pretty good at it."

Angelos even won a trophy (most improved player) and barracked for Carlton. He still does and would have been mightily pleased with the team's much-improved performance in the Australian Football League in 2023.

He put his trophy on the dinner table and his father, who had come home from work, was delighted and proud. Until he took a closer look.

The ball was the wrong shape!

"So the old man put down his knife and fork and put his hand on my shoulder," Postecoglou recalled. "And he said: 'Right, you're coming out back with me.' So we went into the garden and had a kick about (with a soccer ball of course). He didn't want to lose his son."

When he was 11 or 12 years-old Ange and some mates wanted to play soccer at Prahran High School but there was no program.

By that time, the young Angelos had developed a great knowledge of soccer, having sat through debriefs with his father after many South Melbourne games and games they'd watched together on TV, discussing tactics, playing styles and so on.

One day the PE (physical education) teacher approached him and a group of mates asking if they had a soccer team.

They hesitated. "Well Angelos?" the teacher said, focussing on the lad.

Not having much idea of what the teacher was on about but knowing that he and his mates, mostly of Greek and Italian origins, had become reasonably competent at the game outside school hours, he semi-confidently said "yes", so the story goes.

"It looks like we've got ourselves a team," said the PE teacher who then directed them to prepare a list of players, so he could enter a junior team in the Victorian High Schools State Championship. Imagine their shock. They were going from playing no soccer at high school to contesting a Statewide schools championship.

Ange recalled years later: "They gave us this box. In the box was this sleeveless, woollen footy (Aussie Rules) jumper from the year before. Accompanying that were these extremely tight footy shorts, all topped off with a coach who was a music teacher. Upon our first game he told us he had no idea what he was doing, and would often just go sit by the tree and mark homework while we played. By that stage, I was immersed in the game, and said I was going to coach. The most remarkable thing was that I had mates, at 12 years of age, who were listening to me. I would run the drills, pick the teams, talk tactics and do the substitutions. It was a natural fit, really."

His teammates noted Angelos was "tough, skilful and determined."

The boys had one thing in common – they wanted to score goals, they wanted to win, not just the game but respect too.

Angelos knew his stuff. Prahran marched on through the competition in their rag-tag outfits. They won their first game easily, against a team in a nice new strip as befitting a school in a well-heeled part of the city.

The Prahran boys could see the other boys sniggering. That didn't faze them. They would have the last laugh, all the way through the competition to the Grand Final, undefeated, but still without much interest from their school by way of support and kit. At least they got a bus ride to the Grand Final, just down the road to South Melbourne's home ground.

The Grand Final was a tough affair. Prahran won 2-0! Angelos scored one of the goals.

A team of players with hand-me-down Aussie Rules jumpers and coached in the main by someone who hadn't even reached his teenage years were State champions. If that's not the stuff of a movie script, what is?

They may not have won the accolades they deserved at school, but the boys themselves knew they'd made their mark.

Ange re-told the story. "We won the State Championships! I remember the prize: a pennant and Supernaught (Australian glam rock band) album for being man of the match!" he said.

As for Angelos, a career at South Melbourne Hellas at Middle Park beckoned.

A GREEK CONNECTS

An Australian keen to check up on Postecoglou's progress at Tottenham Hotspur was Collingwood star Josh Daicos, a member of the 2023 Collingwood AFL premiership team.

Speaking in Melbourne in November 2023 after a trip to Europe, Josh Daicos said he was mighty impressed with the facilities at Spurs that made those back home in Melbourne seem second rate. He met Postecoglou, whose heritage is in the same part of the world, and some of the Spurs players.

"It was amazing to meet the players and watch them train," he said. "Just seeing the facilities it was the best venue I've been to.

"The way they cater for their players is quite amazing and you can see why they're on top of their game.

"Training is quite intense and you can see the attention to detail."

No doubt Postecoglou would have been happy to host a fellow Melbournian, though probably he would have preferred Daicos was from his favourite team, Carlton, rather than the Collingwood Magpies.

Nevertheless, Daicos was welcomed warmly and was given a Spurs jumper with his name on it from Postecoglou. While visiting Spurs. Josh's brother Nick was holidaying in Greece.

The boys are the sons of Collingwood hero Peter Daicos, known in AFL circles as the "Macedonian Marvel." The family is of Greek Macedonian heritage.

In 2002, Peter Daicos was named in the AFL "Greek Team of the Century," honouring players with full or partial Greek heritage; despite Daicos being an ethnic Macedonian, his family hometown is in Greece and was thus eligible for inclusion.

A downside to the development of children into adults on the playing fields of most sports can be the conduct of parents on the sidelines.

Abuse and physical altercations unfortunately continue to this day as parents let their emotions boilover. Why that happens is a complex psychological exercise.

Parental behaviour at several sports gave rise in Australia to a Play by the Rules *Let Kids Be Kids* campaign to raise awareness of the impact of poor sideline behaviour.

In 2020 Ange Postecoglou lent his name to the campaign.

He recounted how one enjoyable weekend sports match turned ugly.

"I must have been 10 or 11 and the parents started arguing and fighting amongst each other," he said in a video message for *Let Kids Be Kids*. "And the thing that struck is that the kids – us, both teams – just huddled together in the centre circle, each of us frightened for ourselves and I guess for our parents. And even at such a young age it made such an impression on me that the people arguing and fighting outside the field forgot why they were there… because why they were there were the kids, and their kids were scared, huddled together, opposition and our team alike, trying to protect one another."

Postecoglou was one of several high-profile sports people who endorsed the *Let Kids be Kids* campaign. Netball and volleyball player Caitlin Thwaites said children found shrugging off sideline comments quite difficult. Australian Test cricketer Usman Khawaja said sideline abuse often robbed him of his childhood fun both on and off the sports field.

FOOTNOTE: In *The Age of Ange* documentary, made after Australia's Asian Cup triumph in 2015, Ange took his parents Dimitris (Jim) and Voula to Melbourne's Hellenic Museum. The museum had an exhibition called "Through a Child's Eyes", which featured 12 prominent Greek migrants who moved to Australia as children in the 1960s and '70s. One of the people involved was Ange. The subjects chosen represented different fields of endeavour including Education, Sport, Politics, the Arts, Medicine, Business and Law. The interactive exhibition made in 2012 provided an insight into the struggles, dreams, aspirations and achievements of the child migrants who arrived in Australia after the 1950s in the country's assisted immigration program that began in 1952.

CHAPTER 14
DRIVING MR PUSKAS

Ferenc Puskás is revered as one of the greats of world football, rated almost universally as the first real superstar of the game.

Puskás, a forward and attacking midfielder with a lethal left-foot strike during his playing career from 1943 to 1966, scored 83 goals in 84 games with the Hungarian national team and was a member of three European Cup-winning teams (1959, 1960, 1966) with the Spanish club Real Madrid.

He won five Hungarian championships (1949–50, 1950, 1952, 1954, 1955) and was the top goal scorer in Europe in 1948. He first played for the Hungarian national team in 1945.

Puskas led Hungary to a 6-3 win over England in 1953 in what has been called the Match of the Century that resulted in England's first loss in international matches and repeated the dose with a 7-1 win in the return match in Budapest in 1954.

Puskás, born 1 April 1927, grew up just outside Budapest in Kispest, where he made his debut for the small town's football club (known as Honvéd from World War II) at age 16.

On 19 February 1949, Puskás scored seven goals for

Kispest in a 11–3 win against Győr.

Kispest was taken over by the Hungarian Ministry of Defence in 1949, becoming the Hungarian Army team and changing its name to Budapest Honvéd. As a result, football players were given military ranks. Puskás became a major, leading to the nickname he bore for the rest of his career, "The Galloping Major."

Puskás was the key player in one of the most dominant sides in the history of football, the Hungarian national team known as the "Magical Magyars." They boasted a record of 43 wins, 7 draws and just one loss between 1950 and 1956, winning the gold medal at the 1952 Helsinki Olympic Games. Hungary was one of five teams that withdrew from the 1956 Olympic Games in Melbourne, the amateur Association Football section contested by 11 teams with the Soviet Union winning the gold medal.

The team's sole loss during the Puskas era was in the final of the 1954 World Cup, 3-2 to Germany, in which Puskás tried to play with an ankle injury.

In 1956 while Puskás was playing for Honved with a match in Spain, the Hungarian Revolution broke out. He and some teammates defected to Spain.

Puskás joined Real Madrid, teaming with Alfredo di Stefano at the front of one of the most lethal scoring attacks in world football. Puskás scored 512 goals in 528 appearances for Real Madrid as the club collected five consecutive league championships (1961–65) and three European Cup titles.

Puskás became a Spanish citizen in 1961 and represented Spain at the 1962 World Cup, but he failed to score a goal in four matches. He retired from playing in 1966. He returned to Budapest in 1993 and in 2002 the football stadium was renamed in his honour. He died in Hungary in 2006.

How then is it that a truly world superstar of the round-ball game (a member of the FIFA Team of the Century) has been honoured in Melbourne Australia with a bronze statue near the Yarra River that flows through the Victorian state capital?

The answer lies with the South Melbourne (Hellas) Football Club where in 1989 Puskás, aged 60, turned up as coach of the team that included Socceroos Ange Postecoglou, Paul Trimboli and Kimon Taliadoris. Also there were Paul Wade, Steve Blair, Mickey Peterson, and Con Boutsianis. They were part of what became one of the best attacking teams seen in Australian football.

After deciding not to return home after the Soviet invasion of Hungary in 1956, when Puskás ended his playing career he found his way is way into a coaching role at Panathinaikos in Greece, leading them to the final of the European Cup in 1971. He left Greece amid political turmoil that engulfed the country and which had led the Postecoglou family to head for Australia.

Puskás worked in Canada, Spain, Chile, Saudi Arabia and Paraguay in a dozen managerial roles before finding his way to Australia. He coached a youth team in the Melbourne suburb of Keysborough before South Melbourne president George Vasilopoulos offered him the coaching job.

Filmmakers Tony Wilson, Rob Heath, and Cam Fink created a documentary tracing the Puskás phenomenon, *Puskas in South Melbourne*.

During his three seasons with South, Puskás won an NSL Championship (1990-91) two Dockerty Cups (Victoria) and an NSL Cup.

Steve Blair recalled the influence Puskás had on Postecoglou at South Melbourne for Celticway: "Puskás's English was broken. It was very basic. Sometimes it didn't make much sense. He knew words like 'goal' and 'go forward' but he always turned to Ange to get his message across to the players.

"He would convey his thoughts and feelings to him, sometimes they'd speak and then you would see Ange getting wound up and deliver a 'get the f…… finger out lads' speech. Puskás meant the world to Ange. He and his dad taught him everything about the game."

To honour the great man's legacy, Melbourne became only the fourth city in the world to receive a memorial statue of "The Galloping Major", marking his contribution to the places where he was remembered so fondly, the others being

Madrid (Spain), Athens (Greece) and Budapest (Hungary).

The statue was presented to "the people of Victoria" by the Hungarian government in 2017.

Australian delegate to the Puskás Foundation Board of Trustees, Robert Belteky, said at the unveiling: "It's fitting that the world's sporting capital becomes home to one of the genuine legends of the global game. Puskás is by far the biggest football name ever to grace our shores and his goal-scoring record is unrivalled, even by the standards of past and modern-day greats of the game such as Pele, Maradona, Messi, and Ronaldo. Puskás made a profound contribution to the game worldwide, and we're extremely fortunate that he chose to bring his football know-how to Australia."

There's no doubt there's a lot of the Puskás influence in the way Postecoglou has gone about his own coaching career. But it was more than football that struck home.

"I loved the way he thought about life," Postecoglou said. "I loved his outlook on football. His teams just wanted to outscore the opposition.

"It was more his impact as a person. The way he treated us, there was never any arrogance about him. He cared about us as people."

Postecoglou reflected on his years with Puskás: "I was captain when he came to the club… I was only 24 or 25 at the time. We were a young group, but he instilled a fearlessness in us. We weren't afraid to lose or make mistakes. He just wanted us to love the game, enjoy the game, and that is something I've taken into my football.

"Anyone would say his teams just wanted to outscore the opposition; that's all he wanted to do. He goes, 'We will win 5-4 every week and I'll enjoy it'.

"I was a defender, so we copped four goals and I was, like, 'Shit', but he was buzzing, because what a game. They scored great goals, we scored great goals.

"That's just not right! But it was right because what it did was, for us as players, it released us of that fear of, 'Oh, we've just conceded a goal, what a tragedy'. (It became) 'Oh, we've conceded a goal. Let's go up and score two. It doesn't matter; it's alright'.

"He provided that security blanket. We ended up being champions that year."

Postecoglou said Puskás probably was the person he learned most from as a player: "Not just from a footballing point of view but also from a life point of view. He was one of the greatest footballers ever, but he was a very, very humble man and he created an environment in our dressing room where we wanted to play for him. We wanted to win for him because he was such a fantastic person. I learnt a lot about how to create a really good team spirit and environment from playing under him."

Postecoglou had an interesting additional role during his playing days under Puskás. As well as team captain, he became interpreter and chauffeur.

Puskás did not have a great command of English in his early days at Hellas.

It fell to Postecoglou to help him pass on instructions and other information.

Puskás had a bit of Greek language in his vocabulary, picked up from his time at Greek club Panathinaikos. No doubt passing on the boss's instructions helped develop Postecoglou's own understanding of coaching.

As captain it fell to Postecoglou sometimes to be the chauffeur for Puskás.

Once when heading to the airport on the way to a match, Postecoglou was called into action. He recalled the time: "I had the s***tiest car" (a beat-up Datsun 200).

"I'd be literally pulling up and putting a guy in my car, which was worth 500 quid at the time, didn't have a window winder because my mate had broken it the year before, so he couldn't even wind his window, and I'm driving one of the world's greatest players around in this car that's bloody embarrassing.

Things went from bad to worse.

Postecoglou: "I got a flat tyre on the freeway and had to pull over to the side. So here I am, in the club tracksuit, driving one of the world's greatest footballers to the airport so we don't miss our flight, I get a flat tyre, and I've got the jack out and I'm on the middle of the highway.

"He didn't get out of the car! He stayed in the car. I'm going, 'Boss, d'ya mind just...', because he was a big guy at the time – 'd'ya mind getting out?' And he goes, 'No, I'm not going anywhere.' I think about it now... 'Man, I would have done things differently, I would have paid for a taxi.'"

A roadside repair, and they made it to the airport in time.

It was the time spent with Puskás that most likely played a huge part in the advent of Angeball as it has become known.

"We would spend hours together and for me that time was priceless," Postecoglou said in an interview in Scotland. "He taught me a lot about humility, being such a great man. If you treat people well, irrespective of what you've done in your life, they'll give everything for you. He created that as the team environment. We all would literally die for him – we didn't want to disappoint him.

"We had success, we won a championship with him and that's one of my favourite photos – holding up the trophy alongside him.

"It was sad for me that he passed away before I could thank him properly when I became a manager myself – I missed that opportunity – but he's certainly somebody that I hold very dear to my heart."

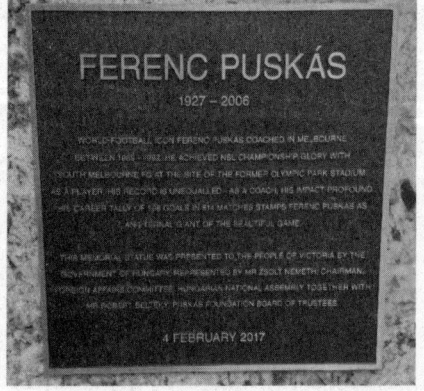

Puskás emphasised attacking

football. Postecoglou: "Yeah, absolutely. He loved his attacking players. He'd tell us almost not to worry about the results, don't listen to the media, just play football for fun and go out there to score goals.

"He used to play with two wingers and he'd tell them never to come back past the half-way line. I was a full-back at the time so I used to blow up about it but then I figured out, 'I'm going to attack as well!' and he loved it.

"He just had this real fearlessness in his approach. He felt we were there to entertain our supporters, we were there to create magic moments because he had done that himself during his career. It rubbed off on us.

"We were a young team and we played with that fearlessness. That's what won us the championships in the end. We didn't worry about what the opposition was doing, we'd just play our football. He certainly was one of the major influences for me."

Puskás left at the end of his three-year contract, succeeded by Jim Pyrolios from 1992-94, then Frank Arok 1994-96 before Postecoglou took over in 1996.

CHAPTER 15
A ONE-CLUB PLAYER

South Melbourne Hellas Football Club was formed in 1959 through the amalgamation of South Melbourne United, Hellenic and Yarra Park clubs.

Angelos Postekos went on to their books as a nine-year-old in 1974-75.

He played junior soccer through his school years then spent two years studying economics and accounting at Monash University.

But by the time he was in his late teens, elite level soccer was on his mind, not university quite so much.

Continuing his association with South Melbourne Hellas, he played his first game for the club's part-time senior teams in 1984.

In 1985 he was selected in the Australian squad to travel to Minsk (then in the Soviet Union, now capital of Belarus) for the final of the World Youth Championship.

His brief bio on the 18-man team list said: Angelos Postekos (South Melbourne): "A mature left back whose form this season has made him a late inclusion in the squad. No international experience but appears to have the temperament to take the championships in his stride."

Ange played his first full game with the team on 13 August 1985.

A total of 32 matches were played. Australia (known as the Young Socceroos) qualified for the finals through Oceania group preliminary matches.

In the finals, Australia managed scoreless draws with the hosts (Soviet Union) and Canada in the Group stage before losing 3-2 to Nigeria and bowing out before the knockout stage. The championship eventually was won by Brazil.

Australia's final ranking was 11, the highest of all the teams that didn't win a match, England among them.

Postecoglou made 13 appearances for the Australian Under-20s team in 1985, scoring one goal (he mainly played as a defender).

Back home with South Melbourne Hellas, Postecoglou rose through the youth ranks to play 193 games from 1984 to 1993 as a one-club player in the National Soccer League (NSL).

In 1984, he played in the NSL Grand Final when for the first time the winners of the two national conferences played off for the title.

South Melbourne took the trophy, defeating Sydney Olympic. Going into the match, South Melbourne committee member George Vasilopoulos was confident the young players could get the job done: "Angie Postecoglou is only 18 but I predict that he will shine in the defence," he wrote in a newsletter preview.

South Melbourne's Socceroo star Alan Davidson was leaving for England. His replacement at left-back was Ange Postecoglou.

South Melbourne won both legs of the Grand Final 2-1 for a 4-2 aggregate.

That was the first of two championship titles for Postecoglou as a player; the second was in 1990-91 as captain of the team. His national-team career as a player included four caps for the Socceroos from 1986-88.

His coach at Hellas in 1989, Brian Garvey, tried the 18-year-old Postecoglou in the midfield in a 3-1 win over Sydney Croatia, the club's newsletter noting: "The goals were scored by Danny Wright and two from Angelo Postecoglou who played in midfield and showed he can be just as effective in the middle of the park as he is at fullback. I'm sure Angie's strength in this new role, will lead to selection headaches for our coach as new signing Harris Michell also had a great game playing at left back."

The year proved one of several goal scoring opportunities for Ange. One report referred to him as a "spot-kick specialist" when he stepped up to drive home a penalty in a South Melbourne Hellas 3-0 victory over Marconi in Sydney. He scored two goals against APIA Leichhardt in a 5-4 victory (including a penalty); a penalty against Brisbane

Lions in a 2-1 win; two goals against Sydney Croatia; the only goal for Hellas in a 1-1 draw with Marconi, and a penalty against Sydney Croatia in the 2-1 preliminary final loss that ended their season after finishing third on the ladder in the season of 26 rounds.

Postecoglou also slotted home a penalty for Victoria in a 4-1 win over visiting Greek club side PAOK-Salonica in 1989, the Greek team's first loss on their four-match tour of Australia. He conceded a penalty in the last minutes of the game.

Postecoglou also scored goals for Hellas in Buffalo Cup and Beach Fashion Cup knockout matches, in 1988.

The program for the NSL play-offs said of Ange Postecoglou: "Youth international and called to the Socceroos by the national coach. A very dependable defender who covers his zone well."

Hellas had finished third on the ladder. The 1988 squad included Con Giatas, Bobby Russell, Manny Anezakis, Paul Fernandes, Steve Blair, Ange Postecoglou, Paul Wade, Paul Foster, Steve Tasios, David Healy, Paul Trimboli, George Kalogeras, Peter Tsolakis, Danny Wright, Harry Micheil, Kimon Taliadoros, Bruce McLaren, Manny Anezakis, John Samaras. They were mostly semi-professionals, but familiar names to many soccer followers.

From 1989, Postecoglou was coached at Hellas by Ferenc Puskás.

Puskás played a 4-3-3 formation with specific full-backs and attacking wingers. Postecoglou built on this strategy in his own coaching, however his use in later years of attacking fullbacks in a non-traditional inverted position differs from the methods of Puskás. (A 4-3-3 formation uses four defenders – made up of two centre-backs and two full-backs – behind a midfield line of three. The front line comprises two wide attackers either side of a single centre-forward).

In 1991 South Melbourne Hellas, under Puskás, won the NSL championship in a penalty shootout (5-4) against Melbourne Croatia, after pretty much having less of the play than their opponents.

Croatia had finished top of the regular-season table, and taking the lead seemed to have the title in their grasp. But they conceded in the 88th minute to send the game into a decisive shootout. After South Melbourne missed three penalties in the shootout, Croatia twice had kicks to claim victory, but missed. Skipper Postecoglou had to convert the fifth penalty shot. He did.

Postecoglou said it was his team's refusal to give up which won the day. "This game summed up our season," he said. We must have a lot of character to keep coming back." Even Puskás conceded his side was outplayed during regular time.

A knee injury would prematurely end Postecoglou's elite playing career at the age of 27.

Years later he made an admission about his time as a

player; as a full-back he may not have been entirely suited to what as a coach he asks the players to do, his right-back and left-back often inverting into midfield. He disliked running.

The NSL went through some turbulent times on and off the field, run by Soccer Australia and later the Australian Soccer Association. The NSL began in 1977 as a semi-professional league.

State officials often were at odds with the national body.

With unprecedented numbers of boys (very few girls yet and not formally) playing the game in the 1970s, Australian soccer faced a bright future if only it could get its act together.

Until 1984 there had been just one men's competition with 16 teams from around the country. From 1984 another eight teams were added, and the competition split into two "conferences," the change brought about to counter decreasing crowd numbers.

The Australian Conference had eight Sydney clubs, the Canberra Arrows, Wollongong, Newcastle and Penrith. The National Conference had two teams from Adelaide, two from Brisbane and eight from Melbourne. In 1985-86 the conferences became Northern and Southern. The system applied until 1988 when it was reviewed.

They were the most obvious changes from the fans' perspective. There was some tinkering with other competition procedures, including the introduction of interstate matches.

The NSL had issues well into the 1980s. Three policemen were injured trying to stop a fight between rival supporters after the July 1986 match between George Cross and Footscray at Sunshine in Melbourne ended in a 1-1 draw.

There was another major overhaul of the League from 1987 when the competition reverted to a single division. The playing of a final was eliminated but reintroduced in 1988.

The 1989 season was the last to be played in winter, the League switching to summer fixtures in 1989, to lessen the impact of competing for media coverage with other football codes, and the effect winter weather was having on crowds.

After the 2001 FIFA Club World Cup was cancelled (it was reinstated a year later and is still held, contested by premiership teams from the six continental federations), the NSL was again in turmoil.

Performances of the Australian national team began to attract attention from overseas clubs and some high-profile Australian players began to leave for greener pastures.

Through the NSL years, the South Melbourne Football Club had operated on a semi-professional basis.

The club was founded in 1959 by Greek migrants after World War II. It adopted the name South Melbourne Hellas in 1960.

Hellas won four Australian national championships, a string of Victorian State League titles and Dockerty Cups (statewide knockout competition).

By 2008, South Melbourne FC had become Australia's most successful football club – four times national champions, six times Victorian champions, participants in the Inaugural FIFA Club World Championships, and Oceania Champions

South Melbourne was chosen by the International Federation of Football History & Statistics as the Oceania Club of the Century for the 20th Century.

South Melbourne's "golden age" was in the 1990s, winning three championships (contesting play-offs another six times), four Dockerty Cups and a Charity Shield.

In 1996, the club was taken over by Soccer Australia, along with clubs all over the country, and directed to change its emblem and name in an attempt to move soccer into the Australian mainstream and away from direct club-level association with their migrant roots.

The club's crowning moment came in the 1998/99 season when it won the Oceania Championship, going on to represent Australasia in the first FIFA World Club Championship, held in Brazil in 2000.

South Melbourne lost all three matches in Brazil, 2-0 to Vasco da Gama of Brazil (which eventually lost the final to another Brazilian team, Corinthians, in a penalty shootout), 3-1 to Necaxa of Mexico and 2-0 to Manchester United of England.

Former Club treasurer Peter Skrepetis recalled the trip to Brazil: "In my 28 years with Hellas, that was the greatest thing that ever happened to the club. We went there with Angelos (Postecoglou) as our coach and we had a very good team, we played against teams such as Manchester United and Necaxa from Mexico and even though we lost all three games we played, it was only by a small margin.

"For us that served South Melbourne for all those years, that was the greatest gift, to have the opportunity to travel to Brazil."

The 2003-2004 season turned out to be South Melbourne's last in the national league.

The demise of the NSL, and issues with financial management saw South Melbourne go into voluntary administration and lose most of its squad.

With Melbourne being allocated just one licence for the new A-League established in 2004, which was widely expected to go to a new franchise, and with South Melbourne in extreme financial difficulty, the club chose not to lodge an application.

By the time the NSL was wound up in 2004 it had been contested by a total of 42 teams; 41 based in Australia and one based in New Zealand.

The streamlined A-League competition was run by

Football Federation Australia (FFA).

South Melbourne was reborn in 2005 as South Melbourne Lakers (their home ground being adjacent to Albert Park Lake) and entered the new Victorian Premier League. Its new name (Hellas had disappeared) and emblem were not popular among many Greek supporters. The name change also drew the attention of American NBA team, the LA Lakers, who threatened legal action.

Eight teams entered the inaugural A-League competition, most of them new: Adelaide United (SA), Central Coast Mariners (NSW), Melbourne Victory (VIC), Newcastle Jets (NSW), New Zealand Knights (NZ), Queensland Roar (later Brisbane Roar), Perth Glory (WA), Sydney FC (NSW).

The league expanded in 2009 with two new teams – Gold Coast United (QLD) and North Queensland Fury (QLD) – with Melbourne Heart (later Melbourne City) joining in 2010. Gold Coast and North Queensland lasted three and two seasons respectively.

By the 2023 season the competition had seen the addition of Western United (VIC) and Macarthur FC (NSW), creating a 12-team competition.

South Melbourne Football Club celebrated its 60th anniversary in 2019.

The club was unsuccessful in three attempts to enter the A-League and also in bids to take an ownership stake in teams already in the A-League. South Melbourne FC (still a semi-professional club) entered the National Premier Leagues (NPL) Victoria competition.

On 31 December 2020, the A-League officially became independent of Football Australia, coming under a new entity, "Australian Professional Leagues" (APL).

In September 2021, the A-League became the A-League Men. The men's, women's and youth leagues were brought together under a unified "A-Leagues" banner.

That wasn't the end of soccer's drama. The APL found itself needing to streamline its structure, staff cuts being the first move from 2024. Two teams, Perth Glory and Newcastle Jets didn't have an owner as the 2023-24 season progressed.

A significant step in the development of the game in Australia came in 2023 with the announcement of a second-tier Australian competition, the NST, to sit between the NPLs and the A-League.

Among the eight foundation clubs set to take their place in the NST that was to begin in 2025 was South Melbourne.

As well, the A-Leagues admitted an extra team, from Auckland which would join Wellington as New Zealand participants. Billionaire American businessman Bill Foley was Auckland's key backer. He had been a big investor in sport and owned AFC Bournemouth in the EPL as well as the NHL's Vegas Golden Knights.

Despite the turbulent times, the NSL was Australia's first

national sporting league, predating the AFL and NRL.

As for South Melbourne, the club continued to be a force in soccer, winning the Victorian premiership in 2022.

All four South Melbourne senior teams (men, women, Under-19 women and Under-21) played off in the NPL-VIC Grand Finals in 2023.

The senior women's team became NPLW champions, winning their fifth title.

The club's application to join Football Australia's National Second Tier (NST) competition was accepted, marking a successful return to the national football stage for the club that's history began in 1959-60.

South Melbourne's favourite son is Ange Postecoglou. In 2000, he was named as the starting left-back in South Melbourne's team of the century as voted by fans and an expert panel.

As a player, he was one of the best South Melbourne players of all time, quick with the ability to attack from defence. He was known as a hard-nosed defender with a knack for outsmarting his opposition rather than outplaying them. He was a crowd favourite, readily identifiable by way of his iconic mullet hairstyle and moustache.

He was a member of the team's 1984 NSL title-winning team and was captain when they won again in the 1990-91 season. What could have been on the playing field is unknown as injury forced him into retirement aged 27.

His coaching record at South Melbourne was no less impressive and set him on the path to greatness.

In 2023, Postecoglou welcomed South Melbourne's admission to the NST scheduled for launch in 2025 with eight foundation clubs and two or four more to be considered.

"It's great," Postecoglou told *Optus Sport*. "It's always been my frustration in Australian football that we're such a small community but within that small community even then we were divided.

"Even from the start of the A-League, I understood when the A-League came to be it definitely offered some really important pathways for footballers in terms of professionalism and opportunities to pursue a career.

"But there was so much history and so many passionate football people who were cast aside at the time.

"It just gives people hope and more opportunity … I think having more opportunities for young players is great."

Most Australian football codes have seen the need for a national second tier competition to ensure young players have a pathway to elite level. The move by Football Australia was long overdue.

CHAPTER 16

GOOD, BAD, UGLY... AND GOOD AGAIN

When injury forced Ange Postecoglou into retirement in 1992-93 he didn't just walk off into the sunset, happy in the knowledge that he achieved success as a player at South Melbourne and for Australia.

He could have walked away. He took a job in a bank and maybe the university course he had started, and the job, would see him enter the world of business and commerce.

He turned 28 years old in 1993 and there was still something dragging him back to soccer. Coaching.

The wheels started turning. Former player Jim Pyrgolios replaced Ferenc Puskás as South Melbourne coach for the 1992-93 season. Despite finishing first and second on the premiership ladder in two successive seasons, South Melbourne couldn't get over the line in the Grand Finals.

For the 1994-95 season, the club hired former Socceroos coach Frank Arok to replace Pyrgolios. Postecoglou at the time (1994) was in a part-time coaching role, at Western Suburbs in the Victorian State League, another club formed by Greek migrants.

South Melbourne finished sixth on the ladder but was eliminated again in the Preliminary Final by the Melbourne Knights.

South Melbourne added Postecoglou to their coaching team as an assistant in 1995. Could coaching be his future, especially for someone with his experience?

Only engaged as an assistant coach, Postecoglou needed a paying job. Maybe the bank would be the place for him after all.

The 1995-96 season was among South Melbourne's worst, missing the finals for the first time since 1989.

Postecoglou was not one to be out "on the tear" with mates. While some players and others in the club were going to nightclubs and enjoying the social life, Postecoglou would go to dinner or the movies. He was quiet and unassuming, according to his teammates.

But he remained a team man.

Hellas suffered an ugly 3-0 loss to Marconi in Sydney in March 1996. Coach Frank Arok lost his job almost immediately.

By the team had suited up for its next game, Postecoglou was in charge, provisionally for the rest of the season. He'd been an assistant on a part-time basis and also was doing some coaching at a private school, also part-time.

He was still working at a bank in Clarendon Street, South Melbourne when opportunity came knocking, literally.

South Melbourne general manager at the time, Peter Filopoulos, recalled breaking the news to Postecoglou that

Arok was leaving.

"I visited Ange Postecoglou at the bank on Clarendon Street South Melbourne where he worked as a teller to firstly inform him of the decision to terminate Frank's contract immediately and secondly that the Board had decided that he would take the reins at interim coach for the remaining three games of the season," Filopoulos said.

"Ange is not one to show too much emotion and in my experience with him, holds his cards close to his chest.

"However, I saw the look in Ange's eyes that day as I broke the news to him, and I could see a person who understood the opportunity presented to him.

"He sprung to action, calling a meeting of the team the following day where he unveiled a carefully thought-out plan for the remaining games.

"He was determined to prove that he should be given the coaching job permanently.

"Ange had enormous respect in the dressing rooms and the results showed this with three wins from three starts as we finished that season."

Postecoglou said that after Filopoulos spoke to him, he walked out of the bank. "There was a queue of people waiting to get their money out," he said.

"I said, 'That's it, I'm just going to go for it.' It was only three games but I thought I'd have a crack at it and… years later I haven't had a real job so I'm doing alright."

Postecoglou had a head start at South Melbourne of course, having the benefit of casting his eye over the South Melbourne up-and-comers while an assistant coach.

When the time came to appoint the permanent replacement coach at South Melbourne, the Board began thinking about some big names, Zoran Matic and Raul Blanco among them. Postecoglou wasn't really in the frame.

According to Filopoulos, the committee assumed Postecoglou would revert to being assistant coach. Perhaps they thought he wasn't ready, despite his success in the three rounds in which he'd taken charge.

When told what the committee had in mind he asked "what about me?" Filopoulos asked him if he was interested. Yes, he was. But he needed to show his hand, declare his interest. and convince the committee he wanted the job and could do it

His chance came at a barbecue arranged by Filopoulos at his home. Ange was there. When the conversation turned to the coaching position the same "big" names were mentioned.

Ange said, "You know I'm interested right?"

He started talking about his philosophy and ideas. Over about 30 minutes, Filopoulos recalled, Ange made his pitch. It was full-on. When he finished the gathering was silent until the club vice president spoke out: "Ange you're our f******* coach mate."

Some may not have been in favour but after some hard talking by others, the job was Ange's. South had a 30-year-old coach, younger than some of his players.

"What he did at South Melbourne was the embryonic version of Ange Postecoglou which has evolved progressively in every job he's had to what you see at Tottenham today," Filopoulos said.

But it could have all ended in disaster for Postecoglou. After winning only one of his first seven games in charge it was reported that there were those on the board willing to show him the door. One report said he only survived because the president wasn't able to attend the meeting (and lack of a quorum) that could have ended it all.

As it turned out it was Postecoglou's good mate Paul Trimboli who saved his bacon apparently, with a late winning goal at an away game in Sydney.

"I always go back to that moment," Filopoulos recalled. "Had he not won that game, with his best mate Paul Trimboli scoring a very scrappy goal in the 89th minute, stealing three points, he would've gone."

And, as they say, the rest is history – back-to-back NSL titles for South Melbourne in 1997-98 (ending a seven-year drought) and 1998-99. And the 1999 Oceania Club Championship, which took the team to the 2000 FIFA Club World Championship in Brazil.

In 1999 Postecoglou was one of four candidates interviewed for the Socceroos job that eventually went to Frank Farina.

"I was praying they didn't give it to me because it was

such an enormous task," Postecoglou told journalist David Davutovic in 2013.

"I ended up getting the Young Socceroos job … I was there with Frank Farina in the early days and I just saw how tough it was for him and you learn from that.

"You learn about how to deal with things at that level and that with the limited amount of time you have got it's really important that you use it very effectively and the best way to do that is to make sure you have your own people with you, like-minded people."

Meanwhile, someone else caught the South Melbourne coach's eye – the club's marketing manager Georgia, who initially observed that Ange's personality was not of a "charmer."

In the ABC documentary *The Age of Ange*, Georgia said: "He was the senior coach and I was marketing manager.

"Initially I wondered why everyone around him and around the club were so fascinated by and respected him, as he is not someone I would describe as charismatic or a charmer. I didn't get it."

But despite her initial misgivings he soon won her over. Georgia continued: "It was only afterwards I got to understand him as a person.

"You would see him on the ground, he'd strike up conversations with kids, he saw how much they enjoyed what he enjoyed."

A romance blossomed and they were married in

GOOD, BAD, UGLY... AND GOOD AGAIN

December 2006.

That was the good news for Ange in the mid-2000s. Bad news was to come, just two months after their wedding.

In 2000, he stood down as coach of South Melbourne to take on a head coaching role with the Australian Under-20s National Team, which he held until 2007.

To use the Australian vernacular, things started to go a bit "pear-shaped" for Ange in 2006.

He found himself under intense pressure to retain his job after both Australian teams under his control – the Under-17 Joeys and Under-20 Young Socceroos – failed to qualify for the 2007 Youth World Cups.

He had an ugly clash with former Socceroos player Craig Foster in an SBS television interview when Foster suggested Postecoglou should "fall on his sword" after the youth team failures.

"It's quite obvious what's happening here, you guys (media) think I should resign, I'm saying I'll leave that decision to the people who will make it," Ange said.

The Young Socceroos missed qualification for the Under-20 World Cup after losing to South Korea in the quarter-finals of the Asian Youth Championships.

Only the top four teams from the AFC regional titles advanced to the 2007 global event, with Australia paying dearly for a first-up loss to China.

That result effectively resigned the Young Socceroos to

second in their group and a knock-out clash with two-time reigning champion Korea.

"If you lost to China, you should have put your hand up and said that is not good enough," Foster said.

Postecoglou ended the interview by saying he welcomed a review of Australia's youth set-up and his position as coach, while adding: "I'll welcome any scrutiny providing it's informed, it's not ignorant and it's not agenda based.

"I'm not going to sit here and take it from people who weren't even there telling me I can't coach.

"The actual garbage I've had to put up with today by coming on to your program is A, disrespectful to me... and B, isn't going to change my mind about what I'm going to do, I'm going to leave that in the hands of people who are informed."

He didn't have to resign. He was sacked as youth coach in February 2007.

Postecoglou said he felt the interview with Foster left him "unemployable."

Georgia said: "For the first time I heard him on the phone really distressed. He was pretty upset and worried about how he was portrayed and what it looked like."

Postecoglou's time with the youth team wasn't wasted. He'd visited Arsenal, Clairefontaine academy in France and Argentina's national headquarters, adding to his store of knowledge about the game.

CHAPTER 17
MEANWHILE, BACK TO GREECE

Postecoglou returned to Greece in 2008 to coach third division team Panachaiki, based in Patras, from March to December.

To all but his closest confidants, that would have been a major shock. Why Greece, and third division at that?

He said: "The reason I went to Greece for a year was because I wasn't going to let Australian football stop me from my ambitions as a coach. It was disheartening because I just felt everything I had done with South Melbourne as a manager had been forgotten. As all things with life we take our knocks and move on, and it's safe to say it didn't hold me back for too long."

He told later in an interview how the experience there reinforced his belief in his coaching ability.

"I was seen as an Aussie and Australian football (soccer) wasn't greatly respected there at the time. It was a great experience and it gave me my confidence in coaching, we got battered a bit and it makes you question yourself a bit," Postecoglou said.

"Then we turned it around, the passion was amazing. When we won we'd be chair-lifted out of the ground, lose and we were escorted out. The coaches cop so much criticism there that it taught me to not be too sensitive.

"It gave me my confidence again and we did really well, we were second. I thought if it worked here, it gave me the confidence to go home and do it there."

But why a Greek third division club?

It turns out that another Greek-Australian, Adelaide-based property developer Kostas "Con" Makris, was financing the club.

Makris was born in Ligourio, Greece, and emigrated to Australia in 1963 at the age of 16.

He started out with a string of fast-food restaurants then moved into property. He still owns property in Australia and Greece. When he took an interest in Panachaiki he saw Postecoglou as the man to make something of the team that was languishing in the Greek third division.

Panachaiki midfielder Andreas Samaris: "At the time we had no clue who Ange was.

"We were a bit surprised (by his appointment) but it was like a breath of fresh air for us because Panachaiki had had two or three projects that had not gone well in the one and half years we'd been in the third division, so we would be expected to lack enthusiasm."

Postecoglou joined in March and moved the club on to a

stable footing; the future looked good.

"My first impression was that he definitely did not belong there," Samaris said. "He was so professional and methodical in the way that he worked – we had not seen anything like it before. In the first days, we felt it was something different and 100% thought it would have success. It was how professional football should be. He is an organised person and created dynamic training.

"He kept his distance but was still close to the players, it was all very balanced and, at the same time, he was ambitious. Everything was clear for every one of us and we knew exactly what we were to do. For a third division Greek team, where usually you just put 11 players out there and play, it made a big difference compared to how we were playing before."

Postecoglou's influence proved a boon for Samaris whose career blossomed, winning four Portuguese titles and playing in the Champions League.

Postecoglou got the team to second place on the ladder when a new investor moved in, wanting to sign new players and replace the coach, despite the improvement he'd achieved. Postecoglou decided he'd had enough.

"Everyone believed in the project and all the players believed in Ange from the first day to the last," Samaris said. "This was his impact on the players. We believed in him from the first day and it was like one of the team was leaving."

The players looked at each other and started to cry when Postecoglou announced he was leaving. The team had just scored a last-gasp 2-0 victory.

"He hugged every one of us and left," Samaris said.

Samaris and Postecoglou would be reunited when Greece travelled to Australia for a "friendly" in 2016. Postecoglou was coach of the Socceroos. They fronted a publicity drive ahead of the match, on the steps of the Sydney Opera House. "I will never forget that hug we gave each other," Samaris said. "When I saw him, so many emotions came out. We both almost cried because the memories came back to our minds. We just looked at each other and we were talking with our eyes saying: 'Look where we are now from where we were when we met'.

"For him to coach me as a player was magical. There are very few people in my life I can share a moment like this with.

"I'm really, really proud of him, we were watching him as a coach having this evolution that he has. I'm really proud telling people that he was once my coach."

Before he left Panachaiki, Postecoglou made sure the players were looked after and that he received the money that was due to him, too.

Arriving back in Australia, Postecoglou had trouble getting a job. He and Georgia had no place to live when they returned, so they moved in with Georgia's mother for almost eight months.

Postecoglou eventually found a role, albeit quite a few rungs down the coaching pecking order, with Whittlesea Zebras in the Victorian Premier League. The team had been relegated and needed a spark. They had lost their opening six games of the 2009 season before announcing Postecoglou as their new head coach in April, with the job of keeping the 2007 VPL grand finalists in the top tier.

With the record he had, Postecoglou in charge of the relegated Whittlesea Zebras seemed incongruous.

The Whittlesea Zebras were a club in turmoil when Postecoglou arrived on short notice. They'd finished last the previous season and had troubles on and off the field.

Club official Joe Sala said: "There was a bit of turmoil off the pitch, and the players and their performances became an easy scapegoat. We were having issues regarding the facility and ground with Whittlesea City Council, and a combination of internal and external factors forced us to remain at the bottom of the ladder."

There was no magic wand. Ange's record there was 16 games, two wins, four draws and 10 defeats, with only 15 goals in their 22 games.

He'd entered an environment where things weren't going right for the club. Steering his young side away from relegation was a task too far and despite his best efforts, Whittlesea finished the season at the bottom and were relegated from the top flight, returning two years later rebranded as the Moreland Zebras.

Postecoglou did identify some talent that proved beneficial to the club and the game.

Picking teams up from the depths was something for which Postecoglou would eventually become renowned, even though he failed to do it at the Zebras.

While coaching the Zebras he ran "elite" coaching clinics for young players. He also became a "pundit" for Fox Sports television soccer coverage and wrote a newspaper column ("On the Ball") for the English edition of the *Neos Kosmos* newspaper, personally delivering his contribution to the newspaper office every week.

IT'S THE ATTITUDE

In his *Neos Kosmos* column on 23 December 1996, Postecoglou wrote about what makes a good soccer player. One attribute he referred to was "ATTITUDE – how hard you're willing to work on your physical condition and on your skills and how determined you are to succeed. If someone is stronger, faster, or more skilful than you, do you throw in the towel or do you fight harder? A great example of this is Paul Wade. Looking at him he was just a bag of bones. Built like a pencil we used to say! His skills were not exceptional and yet he's managed to play more games than anyone else for Australia. This is great testimony to his attitude and self-belief and should be an example to every other player."

MEANWHILE, BACK TO GREECE

In 2009, there was a breakthrough for Postecoglou's coaching ambitions. There were some in Australian football who had not forgotten his capabilities.

A-League team Brisbane Roar came knocking. They'd just sacked coach Frank Farina over a drink-driving matter. Postecoglou was back at the helm of a top-flight club. Brisbane was where the "my way, or the highway" ethic cut in.

Through all the turmoil of those years Ange found Georgia to be his rock, saying in 2017: "I wouldn't be where I am today without Georgia. Through that tough time without her by my side I don't know where I'd have ended up."

He said he wouldn't be able to repay his wife's sacrifices that allowed him to follow his coaching dream.

Ange and Georgia have three children, James, Max, and Alexi Postecoglou. The eldest, James, was born in 2004.

The so-called feud between Foster and Postecoglou was put to rest by Foster when he spoke to UK's *Sky Sports News* after the Spurs announcement.

"It's time for Spurs to have someone who is really committed and capable of bringing attacking football to life and that is demonstrably Ange Postecoglou." Foster said.

"He's done it here with the Australian national team and in club football where he set records.

"He has the confidence, he has the methodologies and he clearly has the experience now to take on one of your six big clubs.

"All I can say to Spurs fans from our perspective from here in Australia is that at each stage of his career Ange has proven his capability to manage the group at the next level."

CHAPTER 18
HEAR THEM ROAR

The good citizens of Glasgow and North London may have been shocked – some even disappointed – by the appointment of the Australian Ange Postecoglou to coach their beloved teams.

Who is he? What has he done?

But once the dust settled it became pretty clear that Celtic and, later, Tottenham Hotspur were getting a head coach with plenty of nous, someone well capable of turning around their fortunes.

He had a four-year contract at Spurs and no one except some fanatical supporters expected instant glory, eighth to first in a season! Patience would be a virtue.

Celtic came to know full well that they had a master coach on their hands and would have dearly loved to have kept him for a few more years.

But here he was at Spurs, one of the most famous clubs in world football. It had been an around-the-world journey for the man who as a lad back in Melbourne Australia had stayed up well into the wee small hours to watch Spurs win the FA Cup in 1981-82, recalling in particular Argentinians

Ossie Ardiles and Ricky Villa.

Postecoglou's journey took him into coaching, picking up tips along the way from greats such as Ferenc Puskás at South Melbourne, then the legendary Alex Ferguson at a Club World Cup in Rio de Janeiro and Pep Guardiola while coaching in Japan.

Now, he had a job with one of the "Big Six" of the English Premier League.

Arriving at Spurs, he said he'd had to be faultless in his career to get to that point: "That's because no one's going to rate an Australian manager, are they? So if I had any significant failures along the way I was never going to get here.

"Part of that process is knowing that I need to keep moving to be at my best. I've got two young ones and they've lived abroad their whole life in four different countries.

"We made the decision as a family that wherever my profession took us, we'd go and we'd experience that. My wife knows better than anyone, I can't resist a challenge.

"That's when I'm at my best and my history is I've never stayed too long at too many clubs… left when clubs are successful.

"All I've tried to do whenever I've been, like most managers, is leave the club you've inherited in a better place than where you picked it up and hopefully make a positive impact."

What does it take to become a top-level coach/manager?

Josep (Pep) Guardiola, manager of Manchester City in the EPL, is the only manager to win the Continental treble twice, the youngest to win the UEFA Champions League. He also holds the records for the most consecutive league games won in La Liga, the Bundesliga, and the Premier League, making him one of the greatest managers of all time.

"I will tell you a secret," Guardiola told an interviewer. "The main thing is the quality of the players. I try to figure out things, but at the end the players... the success we had is because we have top players. This is the secret, no more than that."

Ange Postecoglou, all the way from Melbourne to the "Big League" was going to find out if that rang true.

He always knew he'd be coaching.

"I don't think too far ahead but I knew that I'd be coaching," he said in an interview with *Neos Kosmos*.

"To me, if an opportunity didn't open up (with Brisbane Roar) I would have gone overseas and I'm not sure where that would have taken me, but I would have been coaching.

"There was never any doubt, even at the times that people didn't think I deserved an opportunity. I never doubted that I'd be successful, I never stressed that much about it, I never thought too much about it and it's worked out okay."

There were some giant steps and missteps along his way to the top. His three-game winning stint at South Melbourne turned into four – highly successful – years.

He explained: "I was alright as a player. I played for the Socceroos three or four times, but I was a battler, hard at it, as we say in Aussie terms.

"I always had this thing inside of me that I just felt my calling or what I'd be good at was being a manager.

"Even when I was playing, I was captain of the club pretty young and then I made sure I was always talking to the coaches and talking to people about other aspects of the game, not just playing it.

"I was almost getting myself ready so when the injury happened, I sort of retired when I was 26 or 27, and it was like a nudge for me that this (coaching) was what I was supposed to do and I threw myself into it."

After the 1999-2000 NSL season, Postecoglou stood down from the South Melbourne coaching job to take over the Australian youth team. He was the only person to have been involved in all four of South Melbourne's NSL title-winning teams, the first two as a player and the latter two as coach.

One of Postecoglou's roles when he took of the youth team from Les Scheinflug was identifying and developing future Australian players. The youth squads did win several Oceania Football Confederation Championships and an ASEAN Football Federation title.

But he couldn't achieve the thing that mattered most to Australian soccer chiefs – a place in the FIFA U-20 World Cup.

The South Melbourne Football club noted on its web site

in 2023: "Whilst Postecoglou's time coaching the Australian Under-17s and Under-20s is viewed as a blip on the now Spurs manager's successful career, it was here where he honed his understanding of where Australian football's higher powers needed to invest their efforts and the challenges the sport would face going forward in a country where football is not a priority."

The blip didn't go away until 2009 when Brisbane Roar found him.

Taking the Brisbane job seemed a bit of a gamble, but his success at South Melbourne was a positive.

In his first year he made clear to fans and media that it would take time for the Roar to be successful. Despite his continued cautionary approach, coaches at Sydney and Adelaide identified Postecoglou's Roar as the team to beat.

They weren't wrong.

He rebuilt the side to his own style.

Imagine the raised eyebrows when he decided to dispense with Socceroos Danny Tiatto and Craig Moore. Ruthless? Maybe, but Postecoglou knew what kind of team he wanted.

Former Roar player and Socceroo Tommy Oar spoke about Postecoglou's approach: "When Ange takes over a team, his first priority is to instil his ethos and mindset throughout the entire club. He aims to achieve 'buy-in' from everyone involved, and a significant part of this process happens off the training ground, through daily meetings.

"While Ange is known for his emotionally charged press conferences, where he maintains unwavering focus and controls the narrative, what people often overlook is that he operates the same way within the playing squad. His words are always grounded in logic, and combined with his exceptional level of emotional intelligence, he manages to gain that 'buy-in' relatively easily."

Roar dominated the A-League in Postecoglou's first year, winning their breakout Premiership and earning a dramatic championship win on penalties in the 2010-11 season. A 4-0 win against Adelaide United in Round 13 was highly praised in the media as some of the best football the A-League had seen. The team lost only one game for the season.

The Roar backed that up with another championship the next year. Fans started to call the Roar "Roarcelona" their dominance somehow reminding them of Barcelona's dominance in the LaLiga. There was a similarity – the Roar also developed an attacking style of play, seeds of Angeball if you like.

In the 2011–12 season, Roar became the first team to win back-to-back A-League championships and Postecoglou became the most successful Australian domestic football coach, with four national titles.

The Brisbane Roar had a record run of 36 A-League unbeaten games under Postecoglou's stewardship.

At the end of the 2011-12 season, he left the club having

won two championships, a premiership and an AFC Champions League qualification.

"Another challenge beckons me somewhere," Postecoglou said announcing his departure.

"I'm always on about complacency and not getting comfortable.

"There was something inside of me the last couple of months that got me a little bit restless.

"There's no secret about where I'm likely to end up," Postecoglou said.

His destination was another A-League club, Melbourne Victory. He was going home, again.

Melbourne Victory Chairman Anthony Di Pietro announced the appointment: "Ange has been the outstanding coach in the Hyundai A-League over the past two seasons. He implemented a very progressive style of play at Brisbane Roar and we believe he is the right person to take our club to the next phase of success.

"Ange has been charged with the responsibility of shaping the playing squad to compliment his coaching style. Change and regeneration is what we believe is required… and Ange's track record speaks for itself."

Postecoglou took over at Victory in April 2012, signing a three-year deal. First task was cleaning up the playing list; 14 players left and he signed 15 new ones in what was a complete overhaul.

Postecoglou took Victory to the play-offs in the 2012-13 season, winning a preliminary final (2-1 over Perth Glory) but losing the semi-final (1-0 to Central Coast).

He didn't get a full second year at Melbourne Victory. He was appointed head coach of the national team as Australia set its sights on contesting the World Cup in 2014.

Postecoglou didn't have time to get Victory the kind of results he got at Roar, but he'd set the Melbourne team on a path that saw it not miss a finals series for seven consecutive years. Victory won championships in 2014-15 and 2017-18.

Kevin Muscat was appointed head coach for two seasons after Postecoglou departed.

Muscat, also a former Socceroo, was Victory's foundation captain in the first A-League season in 2005-06 and led the side in its premierships in 2007 and 2009.

After he retired as a player, he worked as an assistant coach to Postecoglou.

Muscat followed Postecoglou's path for several years, also with impressive results. He was born overseas (England) and began his career as a junior in Australia. He played for four clubs in Victoria, and the national youth team and Socceroos.

Playing in the UK, Muscat managed to find himself in hot water many times, suspended and fined for misdemeanours on the field. In his first season in the UK in 1996, he was sent off when playing for Crystal Palace. He also played for

Wolverhampton Wanderers and Millwall, and Rangers in Scotland, winning a treble of domestic trophies in 2002–03. He finished his playing career with Rangers and turned to coaching.

First, Muscat went to Melbourne Victory where he was assistant to Postecoglou. As coach/manager of Melbourne Victory after Postecoglou left, he enjoyed considerable success, A-League Championships 2014-15, 2017-18; an A-League Premiership 2014-15 and an FFA Cup in 2015.

He briefly joined Postecoglou as an assistant in 2017 for Australia's tilt at the FIFA Confederations Cup.

When Postecoglou switched from Yokohama to Celtic in 2021, Muscat stepped up, taking the Japanese club to premiership glory in 2022. He backed that up with another title, the Japanese Super Cup, in 2023.

Muscat left Yokohama F. Marinos in 2023, taking over at Shanghai Port in the Chinese Super League.

Marinos seemed to be keen on Australian coaches, particularly those who had worked with Postecoglou. They signed former Socceroo Harry Kewell as the replacement for Muscat, Kewell having been Postecoglou's assistant at Celtic.

Kewell revealed he'd received some advice from Postecoglou about taking the job in Japan. "He always talked about how wonderful the J-League was and his experience over in Japan was excellent.

"And he always spoke highly enough to say to me that if you

ever have an opportunity, you should take that opportunity and work over here. I was lucky enough to be present when Celtic came over (to Japan for a friendly against Muscat's Marinos)… I fell in love with it here. Especially after the final game the Marinos had, they got in contact with me and asked if I would like to manage their team.

"When I spoke to Ange about his time in Japan, he said 'you'll absolutely love it because the one thing you'll get is a willingness for the players to learn and improve themselves.'"

CHAPTER 19
TRIUMPH THEN LETDOWN

Australia won the Asian Cup – the country's first major title – by defeating South Korea 2-1 in extra time on 31 January 2015 before a record crowd of 76,385 at Sydney's Stadium Australia.

James Troisi etched his name in Australian football history with the winner late in extra-time.

It was a major triumph for the host nation, its biggest in international football. Similarly, for manager/head coach Ange Postecoglou, appointed coach of the national team on 23 October 2013 on a five-year contract, it was his crowning glory in Australia.

He was drained at the end of the game: "I'm no good for words right now. I'm just really just super proud of everyone," an emotional Postecoglou said.

"The players, the staff, the whole organisation, and I couldn't be happier, mate. It was tough, it was a final and you've got to grind it out.

"The courage of players showed tonight, it was enormous."

Massimo Luongo put Australia ahead in the first half of regular time, but South Korea got the equaliser when star midfielder Son Heung-min (later becoming Postecoglou's "main man" at Tottenham Hotspur in the EPL) scored in the dying seconds of the second-half to send the match to extra time.

The goal silenced the crowd that had thought the Socceroos had the match in their keeping at that point.

Extra time was tense.

But Troisi's strike late in the first period of extra time changed the mood entirely as the sell-out crowd erupted. There was no comeback from South Korea.

As Mile Jedinak held aloft the AFC Asian Cup trophy, the tournament had become the most watched AFC Asian Cup ever, since the first event was played in 1956, won by the Korean Republic.

The clash between the Koreans and Australia smashed all viewership, attendance and social media records at the time. Aggregate event attendance reached 650,000. By grand final time, the event had reached a worldwide television audience of more than one billion. (The Matildas would rewrite the records in August 2023 in the Women's World Cup).

The group stage was held from 9-20 January; each of the 16 teams in four groups played three games, with the winners and runners-up from each group going on to the knockout stage.

The Socceroos had defeated Kuwait (4-1) and Oman (4-0) but lost to South Korea (1-0) in the group stage. They then beat China 2-0 in the quarter-final and the United Arab

Emirates 2-0 in the semi-final.

Victory over South Korea in the grand final was sweet revenge (South Korea had their own revenge in the 2024 Asian Cup when they knocked Australia out in the quarter-finals).

With their success, the Socceroos joined Japan, Saudi Arabia, Islamic Republic of Iran, Korea Republic, Kuwait, Iraq and Israel on the AFC Asian Cup Roll of Honour.

The party over, the Socceroos and Postecoglou continued towards the next goal – qualification for the 2018 World Cup.

They failed to qualify directly and had to survive an intercontinental play-off.

Australia and Peru completed the field of 32 finalists by way of the play-offs. Australia beat Honduras 3-1 in the second leg after a scoreless first leg to win their playoff, while Peru beat New Zealand 2-0 in the second leg after no goals in the opener to return to the World Cup for the first time since 1982.

Australia was heading for Russia.

But less than a year out from their appearance there, Ange Postecoglou shocked the soccer world by resigning, in November 2017. He had taken Australia from No. 52 in the world to No. 25.

Dutchman Bert van Marwijk was called upon to manage the Australian team.

Postecoglou didn't elaborate on the reasons for his resignation until several years later, but it was evident he was dissatisfied with the lack of positive response to Australian football after the Asian Cup victory. He probably also grew tired of media people asking about the consequences for himself if his teams didn't get success in this tournament or that, something he'd faced before. People, even Ange, can grow tired of negativity.

Postecoglou said he was left with a "flat" feeling in the weeks after the Socceroos defeated South Korea, as it dawned on him that the code and the country was not responding the way he imagined.

"I misread what happened, what the impact it would possibly have," he said.

"Then through that (Russia) World Cup campaign, I felt we'd just gone back into that cycle again of not understanding what it takes to become a really strong footballing nation. It wasn't just about qualifying for World Cups, it was about having an identity, believing in something.

"That was going to be my benchmark – from now on, don't accept anything less than winning the Asian Cup every time, qualifying for the World Cup and being the number one nation in Asia. And I couldn't find that golden key to open that up."

He said in another interview: "I had this real clear vision about what I wanted to do as national team manager that I thought would go a long way to – not that I had all the answers – helping us open some doors to finding some solutions for our game.

"The reason I was obsessed with winning the Asian Cup was because I thought that could be a watershed moment for Australian football … I think winning is everything. I equated it to the Euros. When a nation wins the Euros, irrespective of how strong a nation – could be a Denmark or Greece – it's a seminal moment in that country's evolution because, all of a sudden, they feel like they've achieved something.

"I thought (that) would then give me the power and also allow me the opportunity and give us as a nation to stand up and say, 'OK, this is who we are now'. I wanted us to be the Brazil or the Germany (of Asia)… and that was my starting point."

Back in Australia in 2023 as head coach of his visiting English Premier League side Tottenham Hotspur he said the 2015 win still filled him with immense pride.

"It's obviously a great memory," he said in Perth. "Even in the qualifying campaign we travelled around Asia. It was a gruelling campaign and we were successful at the end to get to the World Cup and I enjoyed it."

There was still a hint of bitterness about how soccer was perceived in Australia. He suggested that the history of soccer was regarded as having started with the A-League, the old NSL consigned to the memory of those directly involved at the time.

He felt that since the advent of the A-League Australian football had not respected the achievements of those who played and coached in the old NSL.

"It annoys the hell out of me that the two championships I won with South Melbourne get ignored," he said. "Not because of me. Because I did it with people who put blood sweat and tears into it and not just players. Its not like that with the AFL. They didn't differentiate between the VFL and AFL (in terms of history when the previously Victorian competition took on a national identity). They understand that history is everything. It binds the roots in everything you do, yet in football (soccer) we are too quick to dispense with it and not even recognise it."

Postecoglou said he still followed Australia's A-League closely.

"Australian football's so close to my heart. I said after I left the national team job, Australian football and me just needed a trial separation, just some space, because like a lot of people in Australia, it had worn me down," he said.

"The answers I thought were there weren't the right ones, obviously. And so moving forward, what does solve it? I just think we need constant scrutiny. There are some bright young coaches out there, some bright young people out there, we need to start tapping into them, and hopefully they've got the energy to make us the football nation I believe we can be."

THE AUSTRALIAN SQUAD: Asian Cup 2015
Coach: Ange Postecoglou.

No.	Pos.	Player	Club
1	GK	Mathew Ryan	Club Brugge
2	DF	Ivan Franjic	Torpedo Moscow
3	DF	Jason Davidson	West Bromwich Albion
4	FW	Tim Cahill	New York Red Bulls
5	DF	Mark Milligan	Melbourne Victory
6	DF	Matthew Spiranovic	Western Sydney Wanderers
7	FW	Mathew Leckie	Ingolstadt 04
8	DF	Chris Herd	Aston Villa
9	FW	Tomi Juric	Western Sydney Wanderers
10	FW	Robbie Kruse	Bayer Leverkusen
11	MF	Tommy Oar	FC Utrecht
12	GK	Mitchell Langerak	Borussia Dortmund
13	DF	Aziz Behich	Bursaspor
14	MF	James Troisi	Zulte Waregem
15	MF	Mile Jedinak (c)	Crystal Palace
16	FW	Nathan Burns	Wellington Phoenix
17	MF	Matt McKay	Brisbane Roar
18	GK	Eugene Galekovic	Adelaide United
19	MF	Terry Antonis	Sydney FC
20	DF	Trent Sainsbury	PEC Zwolle
21	MF	Massimo Luongo	Swindon Town
22	DF	Alex Wilkinson	Jeonbuk Hyundai Motors
23	MF	Mark Bresciano	Al-Gharafa

CHAPTER 20
THE WORLD STAGE

"Being Australian, I sometimes feel I'll never walk into a dressing room and get that instant credibility because of where I'm from. But that's fine. In Australia, where I've had success, I never assumed that people would follow me because of who I am. I knew that I'd get buy-in if I could provide clarity, if I could put the right picture in people's minds. I've been able to do that. It doesn't scare me. It's who I am."

Ange Postecoglou

Ange Postecoglou took over as head coach of Australia's national team, the Socceroos in October 2013 on a five-year contract. The aim of course was World Cup qualification.

Australia had only ever qualified for two World Cups, both in Germany, in 1974 and 2006.

In Postecoglou's first game as Australia's coach/manager, a home "friendly," Australia defeated Costa Rico 1-0, by way of a goal from one of the country's greatest, Tim Cahill.

The Australia national soccer team played their first

international match in 1922 but had not seriously figured in FIFA World Cup finals calculations, despite some brave efforts.

Making the World Cup play-offs again was high on the agenda and Postecoglou was seen as the man to get it done.

The Socceroos' best performance in the World Cup had been in 2006 when with Guus Hiddinck in charge they reached the knockout stages for the first time.

They were drawn in Group F alongside Brazil, Croatia and Japan. They came from 1-0 down against Japan to win 3-1 after scoring three goals in the last 10 minutes.

The Australians came back to earth with a bit of a thud against Brazil in a 2-0 loss but recorded a first-half clean sheet against the reigning champions.

They faced Croatia in their final group game, needing a point to progress.

High drama saw Croatia twice take the lead, but the Australians remained gallant and equalised both times in a fiery 2-2 draw.

The Socceroos faced eventual champions Italy in the round of 16 and were beaten 1-0 by way of controversial penalty goal in injury-time.

The following years of World Cup action produced little major success, even though the Socceroos qualified for finals play-offs in 2010, 2014, 2018 and 2022.

They didn't progress from the Group Stage in South Africa

in 2010, a 4-0 loss to Germany first up making it almost impossible to contend. (The Socceroos reached the Asian Cup final in 2011, losing 1-0 to Japan in extra time).

Could Ange Postecoglou turn Australia's fortunes around on the biggest stage? Sort of.

The Socceroos qualified for the 2014 FIFA World Cup in Brazil, their third appearance in the four-yearly event.

The team didn't fare well in Brazil, suffering three successive losses – to Chile, the Netherlands and Spain.

Six months later, Postecoglou and the Socceroos pulled off one of the greatest victories in Australian soccer history, snaring victory in the Asian Cup.

But Football Federation Australia and Postecoglou just were not on the same page when it came to changing Australian football.

He was later to say: "When I finished it was good for me to have a break from Australian football – and probably for Australian football (to have a break) from me."

The 2015 AFC Asian Cup win was Australia's first since joining the Asian Football Confederation in 2006 and saw the men's team match the achievement of the women, who won the AFC Women's Asian Cup in 2010.

Attention turned to the next World Cup, particularly after the promise shown in 2014, with Van Marwijk now at the helm. The Socceroos were drawn in Group C of the 2018 World Cup in Russia, alongside France, Denmark and Peru.

The Australians took on eventual champions France in their first game, and despite equalising in the 62nd minute thanks to Mile Jedinak, ended up losing 2-1 after conceding a late own-goal.

The Socceroos played Denmark next and managed a 1-1 draw with another Jedinak penalty securing the team a point.

In Australia's last group game against Peru, both teams needed Denmark to lose their final match to stand any chance of progressing but the Danes drew 0-0 with France.

As it turned out, Peru beat the Socceroos 2-0, leaving them at the bottom of Group C with one point from three games. The path on which Postecoglou had set the Socceroos came to nought.

Postecoglou by then was in Japan.

He had thought he might return to club football someday. But the interest didn't come from within Australia.

Four weeks after stepping down as Australia's national coach, on 19 December 2017, Yokohama F. Marinos announced they had appointed Postecoglou as head coach. He was going to Japan's J1-League.

He wasn't the first Australian to take a coaching role in Japan. The man who succeeded him as permanent coach of the Socceroos, Graham Arnold, had coached Vegalta Sendai there in 2014, though that didn't go well.

"I am excited to be moving to Japan and returning to club

football," Postecoglou said.

"Coaching YFM will be a great challenge and I am very much looking forward to working with the club's players, and young players in particular, to achieve success."

Yokohama president Koichiro Furukawa: "Ange Postecoglou is an excellent coach, with an attractive and entertaining style of football which will suit our approach.

"At the Marinos, we are committed to developing players and Ange has a very strong record in doing this. We are confident that he is the perfect choice to take us forward."

The J1-League was considered the best national league in Asia. Yokohama was a former powerhouse with three titles to its name since the city's two teams merged in 1999; the last title came in 2004. It was certainly a major step up from the third division Greek club's failure where he was involved a decade previously.

The move was a smart one. Success there might even get him the chance to fulfill his dream of eventually going to Europe.

The Yokohama team finished fifth in 2017. After 23 matches into his first season in Japan in 2018, Postecoglou's side had conceded the most goals (42), sat only one point above the relegation zone and was just two points off last.

That may have raised some eyebrows. The upside was the team had scored the equal most goals – 37.

In the last eight matches of the season, the team won four

and lost four. Yokohama finished the season having scored 56 goals and conceded 56.

It was the only goal difference that saved them from the relegation play-off.

But they'd made the J1-League Cup final – losing 1-0 to Shōnan Bellmare.

The signs weren't all that bad.

"We had to make some personnel changes, I knew we would be a good team this year and I knew that we would be exciting to watch," Postecoglou said at the time.

The club that had not won a title for 15 years had every faith in the Australian to turn things around.

And he did in his second year (2019), guiding Yokohama F Marinos to the Japanese J1-League championship with a 3-0 victory over FC Tokyo in their final-round match in Yokohama in December.

The victory by the team that was down to 10 men in the second half meant Yokohama F Marinos finished six points clear at the top of the league.

"We played fantastic football, the players deserve this as they have played fantastic football all year," Postecoglou said afterwards.

"I'm very proud of the players, the staff and we have fantastic supporters so I am very happy for everyone." The win didn't do him any harm either – another notch in his championship belt created an impressive CV that no doubt played a part in his move to Celtic.

A YFM statement said: "The club wish the Boss nothing but the best in the new challenge of his football managing career. He will always be part of Marinos Family."

A first title in 2019 since 2004 for a team that was facing relegation was a suitable legacy and showed there was a place for attacking and aggressive football.

It was no surprise that he was on the move from Japan in 2021 – to Europe, and Celtic. The J1-League's 2020 season was affected by Covid pandemic restrictions.

FOOTNOTE: The history of the Australian Men's national football (soccer) team dates back to 1922, when a tour invitation from New Zealand Football was accepted by the Commonwealth Football Association. Players from NSW and Queensland were chosen for the tour that comprised 14 games, including three Tests. The first Test was in Dunedin on 17 June, New Zealand winning 3-1. The second match was drawn 1-1 and New Zealand won the third, 3-1 again.

Coining of the name Socceroos has been attributed to Sydney journalist Tony Horstead in 1967 when a national team coached by Joe Vlasits, went to Vietnam.

CHAPTER 21
DOING IT FOR DAD

"Κάτω η μπάλα – Keep the ball down"

In a *Players Voice* article while at Celtic, Ange Postecoglou wrote of three words that shaped his football philosophy from the start. They were the three words he would hear his father Jim shout at the television screen as he watched his favourite players in Europe do battle – "Κάτω η μπαλα" – roughly translated from Greek, it means keep the ball down.

His father used to drag the young Ange out of bed in the middle of the night to watch games.

Whenever Postecoglou is interviewed or asked to give a talk or a speech, his beginnings in Australia and in the game of soccer, his relationship with his father most likely will be raised.

And he is happy to oblige because it was a vital part of his development in the game, from child to head coach.

"I've had a real passion for the game from a young age and that was thrust upon me by my father. He loved the entertainers. When I was growing up I had Kenny Dalglish posters all over my wall," Postecoglou said in an interview when he arrived in Scotland.

"I knew the moment I started my coaching career that I wanted to produce teams my father would like to watch. I have a real idea of how I want my teams to play and that's to make sure our supporters don't sit down for 90 minutes."

Jim passed away in 2018. Writing for the *Players Voice* website, Ange paid tribute to his father.

"Losing my dad is the hardest thing I have had to face. When he passed, I told him I loved him and then I said the three words that were more significant to us both. 'Κάτω η μπάλα' (keep the ball down) Dad. I will miss him."

South Melbourne president Leo Athanasakis: "the Postecoglou family has been a family we were and still are very proud to be associated with and we were all devastated when told of Jim's passing. Our thoughts are with Ange's family and friends at this terrible time."

Even before Jim first took Angelos to see a South Melbourne game, Soccer was at the front of the youngster's mind.

It was the common denominator between father and son. Looking back, it was the glue in the bond between them.

"The best memories I have is when you are a kid and you are fast asleep and you get a nudge on the shoulder and you know it's the middle of the night and you kind of know that's my dad and there is a game on TV," he said in one interview.

"You get up and you are sitting on the couch and it's just you and your dad and you think like the whole world is asleep and you are just watching the game from your living room and the Socceroos are on.

"I probably knew back then that football was my cause. I thought coaching was the way I wanted to do it and that's where the passion for wanting to know everything about the game came from."

He spoke of his father's enjoyment of attractive football, revering the great Ajax teams of the 1970s and the Dutch side which reached the 1974 World Cup final. "He hated Italian football – it was the era of Catenaccio," Postecoglou said when talking about his father. "Whenever it came on (TV) he would turn it off saying 'I'm not watching this.'"

His father craved exciting games. "If somebody exciting was playing – like Ajax or at that time, Liverpool were a fantastic passing team, an attacking team, or if there was a player in there that he really liked – like a Glenn Hoddle at Spurs – he would point him out and that resonated (with me). That's why he loved the game."

Attacking football is what drives Postecoglou. "The primary reason I get the teams to play the way I want to do is because I love winning. That's what I love doing. I love winning. I've loved winning my whole career. That's what I crave. Within that context, I want to win a certain way.

"I can produce a team, and I use my father in a

metaphorical sense, but give our supporters a team they are excited about watching and you guys want to talk about every week in a positive way then that's great for me, I love that. That's what football is about for me."

Postecoglou says his father inspired him to get his teams to play the ball on the ground, keep possession and to always maintain an attacking, aggressive style.

"I built teams that he would enjoy watching and that's always been my mantra. I think that he was a pretty clever man and I'll continue to honour him in that way," he said.

DAD'S MANTRA

"When people ask me about my philosophy and who has inspired me, they are generally disappointed when I say that it was no one specific. Not Barcelona or Liverpool or Pep Guardiola or Johan Cruyff. No one who coached me or who I played with. The answer lies in those three little words: 'Κάτω η μπάλα' … my father's mantra."

The *Neos Kosmos* Greek language newspaper noted that from the time Ange was a ball-boy at South Melbourne, to playing youth, then senior football, becoming club captain and eventually Australian national team coach, his father's influence was profound.

In a speech Postecoglou gave at a fundraiser sponsored by the newspaper and hosted by renowned soccer broadcaster

Les Murray, he paid a tribute to his father.

"There is only one reason why I love this game and I'm passionate about it from day one, and that was because it brought me closer to my father," he said.

The difficulty in settling into a new country and culture made it difficult to connect with his father, until football came into the equation.

"In the Greek community there were two places of worship," he said. "Church on Sunday morning, and Middle Park watching South Melbourne Hellas on Sunday afternoon. My old man was not an overly religious kind of bloke, so his worship came that afternoon. When I would drive to the ground with him – and this is me six or seven years old – he literally walked through those gates and he would change. All of a sudden, his shoulders would just relax, he'd be animated, passionate, talking to people and feeling really comfortable. Abusing the referees, abusing the coach, and I just wanted to be part of that. I just thought this was unbelievable, I want to get close to this."

With little access to playing soccer in his early years, Ange played AFL football and cricket. Once, he convinced his father to go to a cricket Test match at the Melbourne Cricket Ground.

"So, we went in the morning and it was Australia versus England and they were batting first," he said.

"And literally there was about ten runs in two hours,

and my old man is going, 'what am I doing here?' The only solace we had was back then you could smoke (in the stadium). My dad was a smoker and at one stage he went to light up and he dropped his lighter. As he went down to pick it up, the only wicket of the day fell. So he looked and he said, 'what happened?' I said, 'we got a wicket, Dad!' Then he went, 'that's it, we are going home'."

> **POSTECOGLOU.** — Dimitrios. Passed away peacefully July 22, 2018. Loving husband of Stavroula. Loving father of Elizabeth, Ange and Georgia. Adored grandfather of Dylan, James, Marcus, Max and Alexi. *Forever in our hearts.*

Cricket wasn't going to be the bonding material for father and son. A mutual passion for soccer (football) would be.

"He really encouraged me to play the game and that is where the seed and the passion for football grew in me," Postecoglou said.

"They are still the best memories I have growing up; going to training with Dad and going to games with my dad. I wanted to know everything about the game. "If my dad was sitting there talking about tactics with the other fathers, I wouldn't be outside with the other kids, I would be sitting there listening. That's what gave me a glimpse into my father and gave me that bond."

Ange Postecoglou carried thoughts of his father wherever he went.

"Everything I do I do in honour of my parents," he said in a *Sky Sports* interview when manager of Celtic in Scotland.

"Particularly, I guess, my father because of the football angle of it. I don't want his sacrifices to mean nothing because I have had an enormously blessed life, but if I can make a difference and his name continues on. He has passed away but wherever he is I hope it feels like those sacrifices he made were worthwhile.

"Football was a connector to him with his past. By passing it on to me I think he felt like he was giving me the kind of upbringing he wanted to give me even though we were in a foreign land. By extension, football became the core of everything we did.

"It has always been the constant in my life. My dad was working, my mum was working, my sister was older. I created this world for myself and it all revolved around football. Even as a six, seven or eight year old, all I read about, all I watched, all I talked about was football."

Postecoglou said he never regarded his roles in football as a job.

"It has always meant something more to me," he said. "We are in a ruthless business but for me it is never just about results, just about winning, it is about putting smiles on people's faces, doing things that are memorable.

"Football has this ability to unite and create something more than just a spectacle as a sport. The club that I started out at, South Melbourne Hellas, was not just a football club. It was a hub for Greek immigrants to come together on a weekend and feel comfortable.

"That happened with the Croatian community, the Italian community, the Spanish community. That is what football meant. It did not mean when I broke into the team that I was playing with Greeks, there were guys from all sorts of backgrounds.

"I love that football did that and still does that. I am lucky enough to have been all over the world and wherever you go there will be two goalposts in the ground. Those goalposts could be two bags or two rubbish bins but there will be kids having a kick. I love that part of it."

His relationship with his father may not always have been easy. In his book *Changing the Game*, Postecoglou said his father was a hard taskmaster, even after the historic Asian Cup win.

"Look Dad, here's the Asian Cup," he'd said to his father after Australia's historic win in 2015.

"And what does he say? 'Yeah, but if you made a better substitution you wouldn't have needed extra time.'"

And speaking in Perth in July 2023 when had had charge of the Spurs for the first time, in a "friendly" against West Ham, he again said of his father: "He's been the greatest influence on my life. He still is.

"He was also a hard man, hard to please. He'd pat me on

the back but give me a smack on the head as well to make sure I stayed focused on what's important.

"He always said, 'You do these things for other people,' and I'm doing it for my family now – my boys and my wife and all those people.

"My dad, my mum – I had a really happy childhood. I know they were working hard to make sure that I didn't realise just how tough it was for us as a family."

Ange Postecoglou never lost respect for the bond they shared.

"Whenever I was in my father's company, whatever I had accomplished, there was a little bit of a part of him that was saying, 'Well, great, but you can do better.'

"The last conversation I had with him before he passed away, I was fortunate enough to get back in time. I was coaching Yokohama at the time. The last game he actually saw we won 7-2 and he would have been buzzing because there were so many goals.

"I got there and I had a good chat to him. That was probably the only time he said that he was really proud of me and what I had achieved. To be honest, I would much rather he was still around telling me that I still wasn't doing enough and I could be better than how it is now."

He revealed his father wanted him to go to Europe.

"He wanted to get up in the middle of the night in Australia and watch his son over here in Europe. I am sure he would have been proud. To be fair, he probably would have been over here," Postecoglou said.

WHERE IT STARTED

"My motivation is always to produce teams Dad would enjoy watching. That has always been the root of everything I have done. I can't shift, because where it all started from is more powerful than any challenges I'll get externally, from owners or media or supporters questioning my beliefs. They are so deep-rooted they can never change."

CHAPTER 22
JUST MANAGING

"As a nation, we like to believe we can take on anybody and anything. We can be smart, but were never going to be passive. And if we go down, we'll go down swinging. Some of the foreign coaches who came to Australia looked at us and said: 'You're not as good as the Europeans and South Americans. You'll probably never be as good. Sure, you can bully teams in Asia, but outside that you have to respect your opponents' That doesn't sit well with Australians and it doesn't sit well with me. I can't start off with the premise that a coach is better than me just because he's from Europe or South America."

Ange Postecoglou

The world benchmark of a football management as a career is Sir Alex Ferguson, a former Scottish player and manager, widely regarded as one of the greatest managers of all time.

He was manager at Manchester United from 1986 to 2013, winning 13 top-league titles. Sir Alex would not have been impressed with MU's start to the season in 2023-24, their worst since 1930, winning only nine of their first 18 matches.

Sir Alex's tenure was the exception to the normal in terms of time spent at the helm of a club. According to a BBC survey, the average tenure for a top-flight manager back in 2012 was nearly four years. Ten years later it was two years and four days.

Comings and goings were not confined to the EPL.

The shortest managerial reign in English football was the 10 minutes Leroy Rosenior spent in charge of Torquay in 2007 in England's League Two. On the upside, he was unbeaten.

Torquay was bought by a local consortium which installed Colin Lee as chief executive, who then appointed former Gulls player and Exeter City assistant manager Paul Buckle as the new manager. Rosenior had only just finished his first press conference when he was told he was out.

The shortest time in charge of an EPL team was the 41 days of Les Reed at Charlton Athletic. He replaced Ian Dowie on 14 November 2006. During his six-week stint as manager he managed just one victory, and Charlton were knocked out of the League Cup by League Two team Wycombe Wanderers. Reed left Charlton by "mutual consent."

Dean Holden, formerly manager of Charlton in the

English League One competition, was sacked after his side suffered four consecutive losses in the 2023-24 season that was only five rounds old.

Manchester United and England legend Wayne Rooney also was shown the door, Birmingham not happy with just four wins in his first 15 games.

It's a tough gig, coaching.

At the ultra-elite level, players know how to play. A coach may pick up a minor technical flaw that can be easily rectified but by the time a player is signed on to a Premier League club, or even a first division team in any country's league, he or she knows the game.

Coaching at the highest level is more about how to play each game having identified the strengths and weaknesses of the opposition which have been notarised, itemised and appraised by a team of specialists.

The head coach or manager then becomes the tactician. He or she also has a role in recruitment. If a team's weakness is in a certain position, then the club will go after the player to fill that void. Hence Bayern-Munich's interest in Tottenham Hotspur's Harry Kane.

The short answer for Bayern's reasoning was goals. Robert Lewandowski left Bayern for Barcelona in 2022 and the club struggled to replace him in the "striker" role.

Goals were also the reason the Spurs faithful would love to have retained Kane. He'd netted 22 in his first 25 games for

Bayern Munich.

It wasn't hard to imagine how Spurs could have been placed with Kane at the pointy end of Angeball.

Player transfers usually come down to price. Spurs were willing to let Kane go as long as they got a good price. He would have been a free agent at the end of the season and possibly gone for nothing in return.

Managers have always faced the dilemma: do you let a good player go for a good price or do you keep him at any price?

There is a question here: do players make managers or do managers make players?

Spectators see the players on the field. They can make their own judgments about performance., They don't always see the coaches on the sidelines who may be ranting, raving or applauding. Or understand why a substitution has been made or a player not selected.

The role of the head coach/manager probably can be summed up in six points.

- Setting plans, formations and tactics
- Deciding who will play in each game.
- Making instant decisions that have an impact in each game.
- Overseeing practice sessions.
- Guiding young talent.
- Motivating players.

A possible further point would be dealing with the club's administrative structure for whom results on the pitch are all that matters.

As has been noted, it is easier for a club to sack one coach worth a relative pittance compared to a player's or team's worth.

In Australia's A-League, Melbourne City coach Rado Vidosic was shown the door in November 2023 just after two matches of the season. His replacement for the rest of the season was former Socceroo Aurelio Vidmar who had previously worked with Postecoglou as an Australian coach. Postecoglou was the assistant coach of the Australian national team when Vidmar was the head coach of the Australian Under-23 national team.

Retired players don't always go into coaching. And some that do don't set the world on fire.

Many soccer fans will know the names of the greatest players, from "way back when" to now: Pele, Mathews, Charlton, Maradona, Best, Beckham, Messi, Ronaldinho, Platini, Cruyff, Zidane, Ronaldo are just a handful of the names that will appear on "GOAT" lists.

There'd be little argument that Pele would be the Greatest of All Time among players.

But did any of them or would any of them become great coaches or managers? Johanne Cruyff and Zinedane Zidane were exceptions, highly successful in off-the-pitch roles.

There have always been great coaches who in no small way have helped players achieve greatness.

These are some that are ranked highly by playersbio.com: Pep Guardiola, Zinedine Zidane, José Mourinho, Ottmar Hitzfeld, Arrigo Sacchi, Alex Ferguson, Matt Busby, Helenio Herrera, Carlo Ancelotti, Bob Paisley, Johann Cruyff.

Some of those names are from the modern era: Pep Guardiola, considered the best football coach in modern football, signed a new contract with Manchester City in 2022, keeping him at the club until 2025.

Others from the list are long gone.

Even half a century ago most of the top coaches would have been from Great Britain. That's no longer the case.

However, if we are looking for the most influential coaches of all time it is hard to go past Sir Alex Ferguson.

During his 26-year tenure at Manchester United, he won an unprecedented 38 major trophies, including 13 Premier League titles and two Champions League trophies. His ability to identify and develop young talent, such as Ryan Giggs, Paul Scholes and Cristiano Ronaldo, was unparalleled.

MU always had a good record with coaches. Before Sir Alec, there was Sir Matt Busby.

He led "The Red Devils" to five First Division titles and the European Cup in 1968, the first time an English club had won. Busby is also credited with developing the famous "Busby

Babes" youth team, which included future legends including Bobby Charlton (d 2023) and George Best (d 2006).

Another innovator in the development of the modern game has been former Arsenal manager Arsene Wenger whose tactics and approach to player development during his 22-year tenure brought the club three Premier League titles and seven FA Cups. His focus on sports science and nutrition was ahead of its time. These are now features of the modern game everywhere elite competition is held.

No Australian coach/manager made into the top echelons in Europe until Ange Postecoglou, so it is worth looking at how someone looking on saw his development, and how he saw it himself.

After playing a game for South Melbourne young Ange would be up late, reading, watching and learning. Watching, right from his first days at the club.

Former South Melbourne general manager and South Melbourne Life Member Peter Filopoulos recalled: "He'd be watching games of football at all hours of the night.

"He'd have papers everywhere where he was accumulating stats on particular players... about what they were doing, how they were tracking individually against their targets, and how they contributed to the collective team.

"He was dedicated, hard-working and a visionary."

Postecoglou once said he thought he was born to coach rather than play.

"To be honest I never thought I would reach those heights (international football) in my playing career. Not that I wasn't ambitious, but I thought it was a bridge too far and I had realised goals by playing for South Melbourne and winning championships," he said.

"I tell players all the time that when you get to the end of your career you will most likely get two questions: 'Did you win anything' and, 'Did you play for Australia?'

"It is nice to say yes to both and it probably carries more significance for me now than it did then."

In July 2023, he was appointed manager (head coach) of one of the most significant football teams in the UK. Was there a key to his success?

He told *Celtic TV* before he joined Spurs: "The one thing about leadership I've come to understand is that probably the most key ingredient is to be yourself. If you try to be someone else, try to do it in a way that was successful or effective for somebody else, ultimately if that isn't who you are, it's not going to work."

Would he be worried about what might happen if he wasn't successful?

He'd said in an interview in Australia: "I made a conscious decision early on that I was never going to be worried about getting the sack, or how long it was going to last. From the first day of coaching, I've always coached in a way that I wanted to, regardless of the situation I was put in, or the external pressures. The reality is you don't get appointed when things are going well. I never wanted to be a slave to the scoreboard, or ladder position. I wanted my team to be their best, regardless of what was happening on the scoreboard."

Advice for up-and-coming coaches? "For every young coach, your number one task should not be to be successful; your number one task should be to have a career. How can you stay in the game, how can you stay in the job for 20-25 years?

"No one is perfect."

And some wisdom for the coaching fraternity: "Find the core of why you want to coach, you've got to find out why you want to coach. What is at the core of why you want to do this? Because as we've already seen, it's not going to be a happy carefree existence."

The BBC noted in 2023: "The 55% of Premier League (EPL) teams making a (coaching) change last season is the largest percentage of the 'big five' European leagues. France and Spain were close behind with 50%, Germany was at 44% and Italy 35%."

Manchester City and Liverpool had been two of the best Premier League teams in recent years, and they had the longest-serving managers.

Since 1955 when Australian soccer appointed its first national team manager, Tihomir "Tiko" Jelisavčić from Yugoslavia, the sport's officials have often cast their eyes abroad to fill the position. Until Ange Postecoglou, no

Australian coach/manager had occupied the top job at a premier overseas club. The flow of coaches between the rest of the world and Australia had pretty much been one-way traffic.

In almost 70 years, Australian officials had appointed 30 managers, some more than once. Five of them were Australians – Les Scheinflug had the job five times, including four times as caretaker. Scheinflug was born in Germany but played for Australia before going into coaching.

Other national coaches have come from England (4), Yugoslavia (3), The Netherlands (5), Germany (2), Argentina (3) and one each from Scotland, Hungary, Czechoslovakia and Italy.

Australia's manager in 2023, Graham Arnold, is the most recent Australian appointee. He also had the job for a year in 2006-7.

Australian Frank Farina (2000-2005) was among the most successful, (not detracting from Postecoglou's Asian Cup). Farina led the Socceroos through five international tournaments, the most of any coach. He won two, finished second and third in others, while also making it to the group stage of the Confederations Cup. His most memorable win was a record-breaking 31-0 win against American Samoa in a World Cup Qualifier. That effort led to a re-think of the format for World Cup qualifiers with Australia eventually moved to the tougher Asian section.

Guus Hiddink of The Netherlands (2005-6) led the

Socceroos to their first World Cup in over 30 years and to their best finish at the tournament after losing to eventual champions Italy in the round of 16.

Graham Arnold, appointed in 2018, has led Australia to the quarter-finals of the Asian Cup and the round of 16 in the 2022 World Cup. It would not surprise if Arnold's name wasn't on a shopping list of a European club. His task in 2024 was to get the Socceroos qualified for the 2026 World Cup via the Asian section.

In terms of silverware, Postecoglou's Asian Cup in 2015 is still on the top shelf, alone.

CHAPTER 23
A PERSONAL PERSPECTIVE

Chris McLeod

When you watch a team coached by Ange Postecoglou you are in no doubt about his emotions.

He is a big man, Big Ange, and hard to miss as he patrols the sidelines, trying to stay within the space allocated to managers. Stepping outside the limits brings a yellow card these days, with another transgression meaning banishment to the stands.

You will see Postecoglou shouting and gesturing. His scowl would send a shiver down's anyone's back. He gets over incidents quickly but will not hesitate to let his feelings be known when his team or an individual player has been wronged. You admire his passion.

Anyone who saw Australia's Asian Cup victory over South Korea in Sydney in 2015 will long remember the day even if, like me, they were watching from afar.

The South Koreans pretty much played all over the Socceroos in the first half, but Massimo Luongo's strike into the bottom corner of the net after 45 minutes on the stroke of half-time gave the hosts the lead. The goal came from a pass by Trent Sainsbury, Luongo pivoting around a defender to fire his shot past the keeper.

Postecoglou, arms outstretched as far as he could reach and a grin on his face as wide as the Sydney Heads after Luongo (then with Swindon Town in England's League One) found the net, was a sight to behold. It epitomized Postecoglou's oft-stated love of goals, especially coming just a few minutes after South Korea's Son Heung-min (now Postecoglou's main man at Spurs) volleyed his shot just over the bar at the other end.

Luongo's long-range strike was the first goal South Korea conceded in the 2015 Asian Cup. Son, then with Bayer Leverkusen in the Bundesliga, redeemed himself late in the second half with a shot on target past keeper Matt Ryan to level the scores in stoppage time, just when Australians thought the game was theirs. Extra time was ordered.

At the mid-way point of extra time, the pictures showed a sharp contrast between the two teams as they took a breather at the change of ends. The South Koreans were down on their haunches, water bottles in hand. They'd given their all. The Socceroos were standing together, taking in every word their coach was saying, ready to give a bit more. They looked to have an edge in fitness.

Drama was afoot as the final 15 minutes began. If Australia could hold on, the game would be decided by a high-drama penalty shootout. If they could snare a goal and not concede, the trophy was theirs. Tense.

The Socceroos went for the goal. After 105 minutes of play, a rebounding shot off the South Korean keeper from Tomi Juric fell to James Troisi who slotted the ball home to give Australia the Asian Cup, 2-1.

The 76,000 plus crowd was ecstatic. So was Postecoglou as he held his winners' Cup high above his head and was hugged by his coaching team and players.

There was an emotional moment when Robbie Kruse hobbled out on to the pitch on crutches and in a "moon boot" for the presentations. He was embraced enthusiastically by teammates. It was a poignant moment. I don't think I was alone in believing Kruse was badly done by when the referee yellow-carded him after he went down injured!

Kruse had missed the previous year's World Cup after tearing the anterior cruciate ligament in his left knee and was out of the game for 10 months. In the 66th minute of the Asia Cup final he went down and was taken off.

Tim Cahill received a knock during the first half and was replaced in the 64th minute. He, too, was embraced by teammates.

This was a Socceroos team with great spirit. I have not seen every Australian coach at work but would not argue with anyone who believes Postecoglou is the best we've ever had. His record speaks for itself.

A PERSONAL PERSPECTIVE

Postecoglou has won trophies (titles) on three different continents, as well as having success in domestic competitions. Renowned broadcaster Simon Hill adds: "Can there really be any argument? Two NSL titles, Two A-League equivalents, two Premierships (1 NSL, 1 A-League), a domestic record of 36 games unbeaten (with Brisbane), 1 Asian Cup, 1 Oceania Club Championship, seven OFC/AFC junior titles… Ange revamped the A-League with Roar, restyled the Roos, and now he is rewriting history overseas. He's ahead by a street in my book."

I have never played or coached at an elite level, nor was I ever likely too. But I have played and I have coached, and refereed.

It doesn't matter at which level, the pressure on coaches – or managers – can be soul-destroying.

Looking back at a rudimentary start in the game, my primary school – a one-teacher version then – in northern NSW (Black Mountain) and far from the "big smoke" was lucky enough to have a teacher who knew something about soccer. I seem to recall he was of Scottish heritage.

He introduced the 20 or so of us to the fundamentals. We knew practically nothing back then – there was no Match-of-the Day on TV. (TV hadn't come to the bush yet).

We may have heard John "Martin" Royal on ABC radio reporting about the big city competitions, bemused by some of the names (Prague, Marconi, Hakoah, Polonia, JUST…). But that was pretty much it.

Our pitch to begin with was the sloping playground, the unused tennis court at one end and boundary fence and pine trees at the other. Grass sprigs had been transplanted to try to create a soft landing. Soccer was a winter sport, so snow was provided from above occasionally.

Our teacher knew a colleague in the city 30 kms away who also knew a bit about soccer. They set-up an inter-school match, my village school obviously outweighed in terms of candidates for selection in the team. In our case no-one missed out. And we had a uniform (black T-shirts). Boots were another matter – not much in the way of soccer boots. It was rugby boots or sneakers for most until mail-order arrivals.

A few stringy bark saplings gave up their lives as dads installed goal posts on a local paddock on the morning of the game. Tennis club line markers were purloined to set out the pitch (field as we knew it) according to someone's knowledge of the required dimensions. A few rabbit scrapings were filled in with topsoil. The work of the dads on the morning of the match was much appreciated.

We learned something about playing the game on the school's playground, with a soccer ball that had been procured from somewhere (possibly even by redeeming Lan Choo tea coupons, as was possible in those days). The game as explained to us: Unless you are the goalkeeper, don't touch the ball with your hands – Lesson 1. You can use your feet or even your head (the latter probably not a good idea given the state of soccer balls back in those days and what we know about brain injury these days).

We had to learn to kick with the inside of our feet instead of toes, for better control. Eleven players in a team including a goalkeeper. Then there were the positions – forwards, wingers and full-backs (defenders) were the basic ones. And of course a goalkeeper to keep the ball from passing between the goal posts (the motivation for doing so possibly to avoid a long chase to retrieve it as there were no nets in those days). We had to know a bit about the rules, corner kicks, throw-ins, off-sides and tackling (no-hands).

Heading the ball was a hard-learned skill and wearing a shot in the face or badly mis-timing a header left you dazed and numb or tingling for quite a while.

The game wasn't really that complicated. Coaching focussed on the basics (no whiteboard) and we had to rely on our instincts a lot. Finding a qualified referee was also problematic as more games were played. Those early days saw me on a wing or elsewhere in the forward line. I managed a few goals.

Our formation was, at least at kick-off, the traditional 5

forward, 3 in the middle and 2 at the back with a goalkeeper although it rarely held together for a more than a couple of passes. Conception of Angeball was still some way off in the early 60s.

By the time we graduated to High School down the highway at Armidale, we found as Ange Postecoglou did many years later in Melbourne, there was no soccer program on the Wednesday afternoon sport agenda in the early years. Rugby was the game for boys. There was club level soccer outside of school, constructed along age divisions. My club was Guyra, just north of Armidale.

Out of those first tentative steps towards a competitive game back in the early 1960s, interest grew to the extent that soccer was introduced more formally at high school level. The growth in numbers was quite rapid. Not all boys (soccer for girls was still decades away) were suited to the heavy body-contact sports of the rugby codes (competitive Australian Rules also was pretty much unheard of in northern country NSW at the time).

It wouldn't be untrue to say that a lot of mums were happy for their youngsters to take part in a less-vigorous pursuit, as soccer was deemed to be back then.

With more potential players around, participation in soccer grew. Still, there was not much to be had in the way of coaching. At school, again as Ange Postecoglou found, teachers were assigned to supervise, rather than impart thorough knowledge of the game.

We had one coach whose instruction to defenders was something like "stick to your man like sh.. to a wet blanket."

Outside of school as we entered our teens there were just enough people around at club level with some knowledge of how the game should be played. We were in a university and teachers college town and that meant there were lecturers and students feeding into the soccer gene pool in sufficient numbers to improve playing and coaching standards.

At high school, our rugby league team had the benefit of some good coaches and were competitive in a statewide competition known as the University Shield.

Soccer also had a statewide schools competition, known as the Tasman Cup, although until the late 1960s it was unknown to us.

When we at last entered, we were extremely competitive in our region and actually progressed to a second round (as a mid-fielder pushing forward I managed a goal in the qualifier). A win over a rival Tamworth team took us to the city of Newcastle, a soccer stronghold. We were clearly outplayed there and sent packing in no uncertain terms (me having moved to a defender's role by then). Our loss wasn't surprising for a team that basically coached itself and was managed by a teacher, against an opposing team where many of the boys already were aligned to teams playing in the city-wide competition at a quite high standard.

There was no "Cinderella" story for us, unlike Ange Postecoglou's Prahran High School team.

I also managed to play for a local area team (mostly high school students) in a "friendly" against a visiting Singapore Under-21 side largely (literally) comprising English ex-pats. That was one of my early experiences as a defender, thanks to the team captain who thought we needed a stacked defensive line. I came off second best with a torn pair of shorts when I got in the way of a burly striker. At least he didn't score, that time.

The point of all this is to highlight the plight and importance of coaches and managers at any level of the game, but particularly in reaching out to the regions.

The job, though stressful, is so important to the development of young players. Natural ability will get you a certain way in the game, but the elite level requires much extra knowledge and expertise.

In my early working years on the Central Coast of NSW I took on playing at a relatively senior level (in defence, as I was considered to have a reasonable tackling technique) at the Killarney Vale club in its formation years. The club's coach was something of a task-master, concentrating on fitness to the extent that most sessions began with laps of the oval (I wasn't bad at that). Then passing drills, positional drills and how we'd combat players in opposing teams whose reputations were known. The temptation to adjourn to a watering hole immediately afterwards had to be resisted.

I almost made it through pre-season with a spot in the firsts or seconds possible. In the last trial game before the season-proper I injured my Achilles. So much for tackling technique. I didn't reappear until the last 10 minutes of the final game of the season when I came off the bench as a sub. Thus endeth the career, although I did make a return to playing the game some years later in my old home town (Guyra, northern NSW), unspectacularly.

While trying to crack a spot in the Killarney Vale team, I was also coaching a team of Under-14s from Toukley in the Central Coast competition. This was my first real taste of the pressure a coach faced, believe it or not. I learned the job on the run, with the help of some printed guides. Playing under a coach at senior level at the same time also helped me.

I was lucky enough to have a team manager when coaching juniors, so the game-day details were handled while I could get the team ready. I had to make sure the players I'd picked for the day knew what their roles were in my tactics. Comparison is pretty pointless obviously, but our set-up was a far-cry from the EPL clubs who travel with around 60 support staff, including coaches. (The total staff at those clubs can be around 300, including security, physios, trainers etc for a squad of 25 players). Or even Ange Postecoglou's team at Melbourne Victory in 2012-13 when as manager he had the services of an assistant manager

(Kevin Muscat), a coach, goalkeeping coach, fitness coach, sports scientist, three physiotherapists, a personal trainer and a club doctor.

My team were Under-14s. I was lucky in that we had quite a bit of talent to work with and we won the premiership in my first year. That led me to be appointed coach of the regional team to contest what was then the Northern NSW State Championships. Again, we had a manager to look after the paperwork etc.

Combining players who'd previously played against (rather than with) each other into a team to face players from half a dozen other teams they'd never seen before was challenging, to say the least. I hadn't seen the opposition players, so working out how to deal with them was a "lucky dip" until I'd watched other games in the round-robin series, possibly just a bit late to be meaningful.

First, what format would we use? I had entered the game years before where the 5, 3, 2 (plus goalkeeper) from the front to back was standard practice. I wasn't happy that we could contain more experienced players with three in the middle and two fullbacks. Five up front seemed a bit of a luxury, so we opted for three defenders including a central sweeper, three in the middle and four up forward including two wingers.

Who to put where? Without moving too many out of their favoured positions, I opted to use my speediest players on

A PERSONAL PERSPECTIVE

the wing and the two biggest and strongest in the centre up front. It wasn't "rocket science." I doubt it was a formula of which Ange would have approved, after all his fastest players at Spurs were all defenders, important when they had to revert from attacking positions. My tactics would not have met his standards of possession control or playing the ball on the ground.

Most of the players came from my club team as they were premiers, so I knew their strengths and I had also seen which defenders could be most effective.

A lot of the teams we opposed seemed to play the off-side trap, so my plan seemed to suit – have the mid-field push or drop the ball forward into space and let the speedy and stronger players chase it. That worked to some degree. We didn't set the tournament on fire, but we finished mid-field after surprising a couple of teams. Creditable I thought. I was asked to help select the representative team after the tournament for an overseas trip. I was even asked if I would manage (not coach) it. Unfortunately, with the Achilles ruling me out of any further advancement as a serious player and my job as a reporter requiring my undivided attention I had to decline. One of my players was selected in the touring team.

And that was that.

I hope that my experience and that of many others demonstrates the need for proper coaching from an early age, for boys and, just as importantly now, girls. Clinics for not just players – referees and would-be coaches, too, are ideal. The game in man regional areas also needs better quality pitches. I would still have no argument with these 12 basic requirements for coaching, as taken from the coaching manual I used in the 70s (can't remember the name but it certainly wasn't written by Ange and it pre-dated *Soccer Coaching for Dummies* by many years).

1. Ball control: Master receiving, controlling, and using the ball using your body.
2. Passing techniques: Practice accurate short and long passes, using both feet and under pressure.
3. Dribbling skills: Develop changes of pace, direction, feints, and shielding the ball.
4. Shooting accuracy: Learn correct techniques for powerful and precise shots from various distances and angles.
5. Heading: Train players to head the ball safely and accurately, both offensively and defensively.
6. Tackling: Teach proper techniques for regaining possession and minimizing injury risks and penalties.
7. Soccer positions: Ensure players understand their roles, and responsibilities, and improve off-the-ball movement and use open space.
8. Fitness: Implement a well-rounded program.
9. Communication: Encourage effective on-field communication to improve teamwork and decision-making.

10. Set pieces: Focus on corner kicks, free kicks, and penalty kicks for goal-scoring opportunities.
11. Goalkeeping: Train goalkeepers in shot-stopping, handling crosses, distribution, and organising the defence.
12. Mental skills: Develop mental toughness, confidence, and the ability to handle pressure.

How many schools even these days have coaches who can impart that level of instruction to players?

Now, there's Angeball, the way of the future.

CHAPTER 24
C'MON AUSSIES

Australia used to be a happy hunting ground for England Premier League recruiters, particularly among the Socceroos.

"Used to be" because at the start of the 2023-24 season only two Australians (three if you count assistant managers) were active on the club lists of the EPL, the premier England competition. One of those was Ange Postecoglou as head coach/manager of Tottenham Hotspur. His assistant was former Socceroos skipper Mile Janıak.

The active player was Tyrese Francois, an attacking midfielder at Fulham. He was joined in the EPL by Adelaide United and Socceroos reserve keeper Joe Gauci who joined Aston Villa, and Steven Hall also from Adelaide United who went to Brighton, in the January 2024 trade window. Newcastle United bought Central Coast attacker Garang Kuol and sent him to Eredivisie (Netherlands) club Volendam on loan.

One commentator lamented: "There once was a time you could switch on the English Premier League on TV and be sure of seeing a few Australian players in action."

It's a different story for Australia's female players. Aussie players in the WSL: Charlotte Grant (Spurs), Sam Kerr (Chelsea), Caitlin Foord (Arsenal), Steph Catley (Arsenal), Kyra Cooney-Cross (Arsenal), Mary Fowler (Manchester City), Alanna Kennedy (Manchester City), Mackenzie Arnold (West Ham), Teagan Micah (Liverpool), Charlize Rule (Brighton and Hove Albion), Courtney Nevin (Leicester City), Remy Siemsen (Leicester City) and Clare Wheeler (Everton).

At the 2006 World Cup, nine of Australia's 23-man squad represented Premier League sides. Four others were playing in the Spanish La Liga and Serie A in Italy.

Only two Australians have ever won a Premier League title.

Midfielder Robbie Slater was part of the Blackburn Rovers side that won in 1994-95. He played 18 times for Blackburn that season when they finished ahead of Manchester United by just one point (there's no finals series). These days you will find him in commentary.

Goalkeeper Mark Bosnich was by 2023 the most recent Australian to play in a championship victory, for Manchester United in 1999-2000 when he was (Sir) Alex Ferguson's first-choice keeper.

Maybe Ange Postecoglou could be the latest Aussie with a chance at EPL glory.

Three Australians were active on EPL playing lists in

2022-23 – Francois, Cameron Peupion and Harry Souttar.

Peupion (the 55th Australian to play in the Premier League) was at Brighton and Hove Albion, starting in their youth squad, but on loan to Cheltenham for the 2023-24 season.

Scottish-born Socceroo defender Harry Souttar had been in the EPL with Leicester, but the Foxes were relegated.

Australian Socceroo (Under-23s) Caleb Watts had been with Southampton in 2022-23 but on loan to Crawley Town then Morecambe. His Southampton contract expired at the end of the season and the 21-year-old joined Exeter City in English Division One. He scored the winning goal for Exeter a day after he signed in September 2023.

Also in September 2023, Matilda Hayley Raso became the first Australian to play for Real Madrid in the La Liga F competition.

The days of Cahill, Emerton, Kewell, Viduka and Schwarzer, household names both in Australia and England, had become distant memories. Long gone from the pitches too by 2023 were the more recent "big names" – Craig Moore, Aaron Mooy, Kevin Muscat, Lucas Neill and Paul Okon. The new crop, as small as it was, had a lot to live up to.

There were no Australian players on the Tottenham Hotspur books in 2023. A handful had turned out for the Lilywhites in previous years: Mark Viduka, Mile Jedinak (now an assistant to Ange Postecoglou), John Aloisi, Paul Allen, Terry Naylor, and David Howells.

Big news in Australian football in November 2023 was the signing of Nestory Irankunda (Tanzania-born of Burundi heritage) from Adelaide United in the A-League for a seven-figure sum by German giants Bayern Munich. He was to join them in 2024. Saudi Arabian side Al Wehda recruited Johnny Warren medallist Craig Goodwin.

Other Australians with coaching jobs overseas included: Joe Montemurro (Juventus Women – Serie A Women, head coach); Alen Stajcic (Philippines – International, head coach); Tanya Oxtoby (Chelsea Women – FA Women's Super League, assistant and Northern Ireland women's team); Peter Cklamovski (Montedio Yamagata – J2 League, head coach); John Hutchinson (El Paso Locomotive – USL Championship, head coach/technical director); Michael Valkanis (KAS Eupen – Belgian Pro League, assistant coach); Shaun Ontong (Yokohama F.Marinos – J1-League, assistant coach); David Zdrilic (Genoa – Serie A, likely assistant coach); Belinda Wilson (FIFA, technical development manager).

Australians Graham Arnold, Tom Sermani, Ron Smith and Aurelio Vidmar also had overseas coaching experience.

There is another name to add the list of Australians in the EPL, though not a player or coach.

One of the top English referees is Australian Jarred Gillett, who previously officiated in the A-League in Australia. He was promoted to the EPL in the 2021-2022 season.

He was in charge of the Spurs-Nottingham Forest clash

on 16 December 2023 that saw Yves Bissouma get a straight a red card for a clumsy tackle, and missing from the Spurs line-up for several matches. A yellow card to Destinee Udogie meant another player would be missing from the Spurs lineup for the next match.

Gillett made his English debut as a whistle-blower on 22 April 2019 after he refereed 16 Australian A-League matches. He had also refereed a "friendly" between Iraq and Argentina.

He made his EPL debut on 25 September 2021, becoming the second person born outside of the British Isles to referee a Premier League game, officiating over a 1-1 draw between Watford and Newcastle United.

The lack of Premier League players is not to say Australians aren't in demand in lower leagues in the UK and the rest of the world.

The website *au.soccerway.com* listed 217 Australians on club lists throughout the world in 2023.

Thirty of them were in England, ranging from non-professional leagues through lower divisions to the EPL, mostly in the English Football League which comprises the Championship, League One and League Two competitions.

Another 16 Australians were playing or coaching in the US,

14 in Scotland, 11 in India, 10 in each of Croatia and Japan (including Kevin Muscat), 9 in New Zealand and 7 in Norway.

The rest: Spain 6, Italy 2, Germany 6, France 6, The Netherlands 6, Austria 3, Bangladesh 1, Belgium 5, Bulgaria 1, Canada 2, Cook Islands 1, Czech Republic 1, Denmark 5, Finland 4, Greece 2, Hong Kong 2, Iceland 3, Indonesia 1, Israel 1, South Korea 6, Luxembourg 1, Malaysia 4, Malta 1, Montenegro 3, North Macedonia 1, Poland 1, Serbia 3, Singapore 3, Slovenia 1, Sweden 1, Thailand 1, Turkey 1, Uruguay 1, Vietnam 4 and Wales 3.

Postecoglou's arrival at Spurs via Celtic seems to have aroused increased interest in Australian coaches and players, particularly in Scotland.

Socceroos coach Graham Arnold revealed he was approached by Scottish Premier League club Hibernian but declined. Next on Hibs' shopping list appeared to be Central Coast Mariners premiership-winning coach in the A-League, Nick Montgomery (a Scot), terms reportedly agreed in September 2023.

Joe Marston (7 January 1926 – 29 November 2015) was the first Australian to play professionally in the UK. He represented Australia and also coached the national team but made his name with English club Preston North End.

Signed in 1950, he was not only the first Australian to play in England but also the first Australian to play in an FA Cup final, being presented to the Queen Mother in 1954 at

Wembley. West Bromwich Albion defeated Preston North End 3-2.

He made 154 appearances for the club and was picked for the English League in a match against the Scottish League.

He was awarded the MBE, the Australian Sports Medal and inducted into the Football Australia Hall of Fame.

These days, the best player in the A-League grand final is awarded the Joe Marston Medal.

Harry Kewell is probably the highest rated Australian player to appear in the EPL.

In 2012, Kewell was named Australia's greatest footballer in a vote by Australian fans, players and media.

He wasn't in an EPL championship-winning team but played five Champions League finals, four with Liverpool and one with Leeds.

Kewell was also one of only a handful of Australians – men or women – to have ever played in an FA Cup final. The others include Joe Marston, Craig Johnston, Taryn Rockall, Tim Cahill, Mile Jedinak, Hayley Raso, Alanna Kennedy, Steph Catley, Caitlin Foord, and Sam Kerr.

Australian men have played in six FA Cup finals for a win-loss record of 2-4.

Craig Johnston scored on 10 May 1986 as Liverpool defeated Everton 3-1 to become the first Aussie to earn a winner's medal in the oldest national football competition in the world.

Harry Kewell also claimed an FA Cup winner's medal, in 2006 (he was subbed off with injury in the 46th minute) when Liverpool and West Ham drew 3-3 in ordinary time, Liverpool going on to win the penalty shoot-out 3-1.

Kewell had an impressive international career and won 58 caps for Australia, scoring 17 goals over his 16 years in the Socceroos.

He represented Australia at the 1995 FIFA Under-17 World Championship, the 1997 FIFA Confederations Cup, where Australia finished runners-up, the 2004 OFC Nations Cup, which Australia claimed for the fourth time, the 2006 FIFA World Cup, the 2007 AFC Asian Cup, the 2010 FIFA World Cup and the 2011 AFC Asian Cup, where Australia finished runners-up.

Kewell played for three seasons in the Leeds United youth team, and at age 17 was promoted to the first team where he helped Leeds to the semi-final of the UEFA Champions League in 2000–01.

He scored 45 goals in more than 180 appearances for Leeds over eight years.

Rejecting more financially enticing offers, Kewell moved to the club he supported as a boy, Liverpool, for the start of the 2003-04 season.

He played the 2008-09 seasons with Galatasaray in the Turkish Super Lig and went on to play for Melbourne Victory (2011-12), Al-Gharafa in the Qatar Stars League

(2012-13), then finally, Melbourne Heart, now Melbourne City (2013-14). He retired in 2014.

Kewell's final Socceroos appearance was in 2012, a year before Postecoglou took charge.

Kewell had a couple of unsuccessful coach/manager stints (another victim of "sack the coach" syndrome) in minor leagues in the UK, including the Crawley Town, Notts County, Oldham Athletic and Barnet teams

He joined Ange Postecoglou's "backroom" staff at Celtic in the Scottish League in 2022 before moving to Japan in 2023. Kewell described Postecoglou as Australia's greatest ever coach.

Mile Jedinak was the first Australian to captain a team (Crystal Palace) in an FA Cup final, losing 2-1 to Wayne Rooney's MU in 2016. Kevin Muscat almost had that honour in 2004 but was injured in the semi-final and missed the game.

Sydney-born Michael John "Mile" Jedinak is a former captain of the Australian national team, including for the 2015 Asian Cup victory. He played for Sydney United and Central Coast mariners in Australian national leagues before a season at Turkish club Gençlerbirliği before going on to Crystal Palace and Aston Villa in the EPL.

He was loan development manager at Aston Villa in 2021 before being appointed to a coaching role with Aston Villa's academy, a role that took him to Glasgow to see Ange

Postecoglou at work.

In November 2017, Jedinak's hat-trick secured a 3-1 (aggregate) win to earn Postecoglou's Socceroos a World Cup berth in 2018.

That was the end of the Jedinak-Postecoglou association until Jedinak visited Celtic's base in Glasgow in May 2022 and they caught up.

"When I look back on it, we hadn't seen each other since the night we qualified for the World Cup. It was his last game as Socceroos coach and looking back on it, it was my last game in Australia," Jedinak said in Glascow.

"I was really looking forward to (seeing him), and it was great. A lot of time has passed. A lot of memories. But just seeing how he is doing, and how he's getting on, a lot of admiration there.

"He came in (as Socceroos coach) and knew that the job was going to be tough, but never showed that. Always instilled everybody with the belief of what he was trying to do and that resonated with all the players. And once we started to get results came the Asian Cup and after that, we just went on the journey together.

"Everyone went on that journey and you wanted to be on that journey. Right the way through. I'm glad that it ended in another World Cup qualification and he went with our best wishes after that, because you've got aspirations of going and managing at the top level. He's got there now, so looking back, it was the decision he had to make.

"The biggest compliment I can pay to him is I know what he's like, how he works, what he wants to do and how he sees the game.

"I just have the biggest smile on my face because I think that's something that is the best acknowledgement. You don't have to go and tell people, (when people ask) 'what he's going to be like?'. I always tell people, just wait and see. You'll see it. It's going to be so evident."

Spurs also have another "Down Under" connection. New Zealander Geoff Scott is head of medicine-and sports science at the club. He's been there for about 20 years.

CHAPTER 25
THE 'BIG ANGE' WE KNOW

"Ange was no ordinary footballer. Even from his younger days, he showcased maturity and wisdom that belied his age. By the age of 24. Captaining South Melbourne was not just a position for him; it was responsibility he carried with great seriousness."

Peter Filopoulos, former general manager of South Melbourne, more recently Head of Marketing, Communications and Corporate Affairs of Football Australia.

Peter Filopoulos has more than 25 years of experience in sports administration, going back to the days as general manager at South Melbourne FC where he worked with Postecoglou for just on six years.

He remembers the young Postecoglou's thirst for knowledge. "It struck me how he never settled for what he knew. His thirst for knowledge had him seeking wisdom from iconic leaders in football, from Liverpool legends Bob Paisley and Bill Shank to global coaching giants," Filopoulos said. "This commitment to growth is evident in how extensively he read and learned about prominent coaches across the globe.

"His dedication to South Melbourne was something I personally admired. Ange wasn't just involved in the club; he lived its history and always advocated for it to be recognised and honoured.

"When he shifted gears from player to assistant coach, it was… more than a mere change of life. His commitment was unyielding. Drawing from his experiences under greats like Frank Arok and Ferenc Puskas, he demonstrated a laser-sharp focus in understanding the nuances of leadership both on and off the field.

"This focus was accompanied by high expectations, both of himself and those around him, which is a testament to his commitment to excellence."

One incident in particular came to mind.

After a South Melbourne 3-0 loss away to Marconi (Sydney) in March 1996, Frank Arok was relieved of his duties and Postecoglou, then an assistant, was put in charge on an interim basis for the remaining three games of the season.

"I remember getting the long bus trip to the airport from Fairfield (Sydney suburb) and Frank had slumped in his seat and was just sulking a little bit. The players started to misbehave and were bantering. It was as if they had won 3-0, not lost 3-0. I could see Ange to the right of me was just not amused at all, I'm sitting at the front of the bus as the official. And it got to the stage that it was out of control on the bus,"

Filopoulos recalled.

"He went up to the front of the bus and picked up the microphone. He said, 'You listen to me, you blokes'. It fell silent and he said to them, 'I've played for this club from under eights, right through to every level of South Melbourne, I've worn this jersey for every team age group, to the seniors, I captained this club and won championships.If you want to muck around, no problem, we lost 3-0 but I just want to tell you my perspective, today was the worst performance I've seen of any, any South Melbourne team of any age group in my entire career. So if you guys are happy with yourselves, and you want to muck around on the bus, why don't you just reflect on the disgraceful performance and how you disgraced the team jersey today and the club'.

"That was it. There was silence for the rest of the bus trip. And then we got to the airport. And there was all this shuffling of the boarding passes. No one wanted to sit next to Ange."

Postecoglou was well aware of the reaction. He wrote in his book *Changing the Game*: "When the boarding passes were being distributed the players would jostle to make sure they weren't sitting next to me. Invariably that pleasure would fall the way of one of the hapless young guys. Their reward was to sit in stoney silence next to me. They'd look straight ahead for the whole flight. The 4 hour trip west to play Perth Glory always produced the biggest scramble in the departure lounge."

Filopoulos was on the "ground floor" of Postecoglou's

coaching career. In fact, he was instrumental in the ex-captain's first permanent appointment to the coaching ranks when Arok left.

When Postecoglou was being touted for a move to Celtic, Peter Smith of *The Scotsman* newspaper sought out Filopoulos to ask what should be expected of the Australian.

"The guy has 25 years of experience at the sharp end," Filopoulos told him. "I hear it said he will need time, and he does look to reshape comprehensively. But his mindset is that every football job has to be two-track: as you remodel behind the scenes, you have to win, and win with finesse.

"He has worked for clubs expected to succeed in every game and that wouldn't trouble him at Celtic. If he does get the job, he will feed off being backed into a corner, having doubts expressed. That is when he works best.

"He is always challenged by his environment, but he will also challenge that environment: challenge not only players but directors and the entire culture, because he constantly strives to upscale parameters."

Filopoulos said in his 30 years working in sport he had never encountered a coach as meticulous in his preparation.

"To explain how highly I rate him, I would make this claim. He was linked with the Sunderland job in late 2017. If he had been appointed then, they could be in the Premier League now, not the third tier," he said.

Filopoulos spoke further about what it was like talking

football with Postecoglou.

"Every time I spoke to Ange, I felt like I was educated about football," he said. " Because I was an administrator. I never played at a high level. I was a little bit more educated about South Melbourne's history and he was very proud of South Melbourne history, the club and he always had these really big aspirations for the club, but also big aspirations for football in Australia as he still does."

Those who have known Ange Postecoglou for many years don't see his rise to the elite level of managerial responsibility as unexpected.

While injury put a premature end to what could have been a great career as a player, coaching was a logical step.

Even as a young lad, his knowledge of the game was above that of his contemporaries, thanks largely to his father. Discussion of tactics and analysis of games was part of his upbringing.

It was no surprise to see him enter the coaching ranks as an assistant at his beloved South Melbourne. Even then it was obvious to many that he was going somewhere.

Those who remember those days spoke highly of Postecoglou when he was announced as the "boss" at Celtic then Tottenham Hotspur.

His appointment at Celtic back in 2021 had the UK soccer media trying to find out more about the big man who'd stepped into their world. The interest heightened when he won the job at Spurs.

The media – and the fans – wanted to know more about Postecoglou. Who, what, where, how?

A lot of that information would come from friends and associates who had known him from the very start of his career.

In various media interviews, those people pointed to the attributes likely to make him successful at the highest level.

For some, he had influenced their careers. For others, it was admiration of his dedication and integrity.

Steve Blair, who migrated to Melbourne when he was 11 years old, spent 14 years (1980-93) at South Melbourne Hellas, all of his career from when he was 17. In every game Ange played for South Melbourne, Blair also played.

"We've won championships together, we've lost together, we both represented Australia, we did everything together. We are very tight, really close pals," Blair said.

The two remain mates and Blair says Postecoglou is intensely loyal and has never forgotten his friends on his way up the footballing ladder.

Blair said Postecoglou "learned at the feet of one of the best". His mate was "like a sponge" when he absorbed information.

"From the Puskas influence to all the Scottish boys that he played with in the South Melbourne team and the players he competed against, he took it all in. He stored it all away and kept it for the day he would be given the opportunity of a lifetime," Blair said.

Another with first-hand knowledge of Postecoglou is Australian Socceroos manager Graham Arnold.

In 2023 Arnold was linked to a possible move to a European Club (Hibernian in Scotland among them) but decided to stay put in Australia, saying, "It was an honour that they rang me and offered me the job, but I've got a job to do here," referring to Australia's tilt at the Asian Cup and the build-up to the next World Cup in the Americas in 2026.

At a press conference in June 2023 to announce his team for an international match against Argentina (the Socceroos lost 2-0) the questioning turned to Arnold's thoughts on the new boss at Spurs.

Question: Arnie, a huge story developing in Australian football with Ange going to Tottenham Hotspur. You had some great battles with him over the years…

Graham Arnold: "I didn't win many!"

Q: Did you think back then his football was capable of reaching the heights it is now, and also how do you think he will go in this job if he takes it?

GA: "Mentally, probably years ago and I worked as his assistant in 2002 I think it was at the Under-20 World Cup in Dubai, just from working with him there I could see the obsession. I think that's the right word. Obsession of football; he is just totally obsessed with the game. It is his life.

"(I) always knew that he had that mentality of where he wanted to go, that was to the top. He had a few setbacks but that is coaching. You learn from those types of setbacks and Ange has always been someone that has always (been) so determined to prove the doubters wrong.

"I think that, in a lot ways, is his motivation. I'm just so happy for him.

"Honestly, me and Ange are mates, but we were competitors against each other. To see him doing what he's doing is just brilliant. Not only for himself."

Q: There is him, Kevin Muscat in Yokohama, Michael Valkanis has just taken a job in Israel, Joe Montemurro in the women's game, you just got a big wrap recently from Lionel Scaloni, what does all this say about…

GA: "We might not be so bad, eh?"

Q: What does all this say about not only the quality of Australian coaches but also the perception of Australian coaches in Australia versus overseas? It seems like overseas is waking up to the fact that we've got some good managers here.

GA: "I think that one of the hardest things to do… when we played Chelsea with Sydney FC and Jose Mourinho came out, he asked (me) how the salary cap worked. He said, 'how much is it?' At the time, I think it was about $2.1 million and he was like, 'woah, how can you coach with that?'

"We've got a hard way for coaching in Australia; there's only basically 12 jobs professionally plus the national team, so it's a hard gig.

"I spent the back end of my playing career overseas and a

lot of my mindset is I want to help Australian kids but with a lot of the younger coaches – I'm bringing Ufuk Talay into this camp to give him an opportunity to experience, he's not staying, he has to go coach – we've got some great young coaches in the A-League and overseas. Kevin Muscat is doing fantastic. These guys will end up overseas.

"Ange is the leader of that pathway. It was like all those years ago in playing with Craig Johnston the first real Australian to go overseas and he led the pathways for myself, (Eddie) Krncevic, (David) Mitchell, (Robbie) Slater and (Frank) Farina.

"You need someone to open the eyes of people around the world to say, 'oh, the Australian coaches might not be so bad'. Ange is doing that and has done that fantastically well for all of us."

Q: You know a lot about the big bad world of coaching, can you detail how incredible an achievement it is from Ange to go from someone who doesn't have a playing career in Europe, doesn't have a brand, to go from where he was to go to where he will probably be tonight our time? How incredible an achievement is that?

GA: "It's his obsession. He would sit and watch football all day, I'm not like that. I can't watch it all day. He is obsessed with his career in a lot of ways, his family and his job.

"When I went to Celtic for the day or two, he was just full-on all day.

"On the tactical side of things he's not relying on other people to tell him what to do because he's got that nous. On the managerial side, he knows man management, he knows how to get the best out of people and motivate people. Sometimes, a lot of managers leave the coaching to someone else to do and they're playing the way of that other coach. With Ange, it is his way. It is fantastic.

"Look at the way he coached with Brisbane, look at the way he played earlier on.

"I think he finished his career early with a knee injury and he had the luxury at that time, young, working with Frank Arok and (Ferenc) Puskas. He has learned from two very experienced European coaches straight away.

"Because we're coaching with a salary capped system, we've had to do a lot more work, a lot harder work and focus on the tactical side more than ever. Ange has always been extremely motivated to do it his way and its working well."

Postecoglou's former teammate at South Melbourne, Mike Petersen, was another who could provide an insight into his rise through the world coaching ranks.

Michael "Mickey" Petersen was a noted midfielder. He began his career with Port Melbourne juniors, later joining Heidelberg United.

Petersen, Australian-born of Danish heritage, represented Australia in the Socceroos from 1985 to 1992. The midfielder also played nine seasons at South Melbourne and 171 National

Soccer League games. He played in NSL championship teams with Brunswick and South Melbourne before a stint with Ajax Amsterdam (Holland) from 1987. He was a member of the South Melbourne Football Club Team of the Century.

Petersen and Postecoglou both played for South Melbourne and began their international careers as teenagers under Frank Arok. Petersen was assistant coach to Postecoglou with the Young Socceroos in 2005. They remain good friends.

WAIT FOR IT...

"I believe that Ange's finest hour is yet to be written and Australian football should be excited," Mike Petersen in an interview with David Davutovic in Melbourne's *Herald Sun* newspaper in October, 2013.

During his football career, Petersen played 50 matches for the Socceroos, including 32 "A" internationals and scored four goals. He is an inductee of the Football Federation Australia Hall of Fame, joining Postecoglou on the list of "greats".

Petersen was an "eyewitness" to Postecoglou's progress to the top ranks of coaching. They played together at South Melbourne when Postecoglou was captain; Postecoglou coached Petersen at South Melbourne; Petersen took over as coach from Postecoglou in 2000.

The pair were good friends throughout their careers. The friendship remained, even though Postecoglou the coach was the one to tap Petersen the player on the shoulder in 1997 and tell him his playing days at South Melbourne were at an end.

The pair first encountered each other in Under-10s competition, Postecoglou with South Melbourne Hellas and Petersen with Port Melbourne.

Petersen joined Postecoglou at South Melbourne in late 1989, via Heidelberg and Brunswick in Victoria and Ajax in the Netherlands.

"It was clear from a young age he had leadership qualities, he was captain of South Melbourne from 21," Petersen said.

"He was underestimated (as a player) but obviously he got wiped out pretty young at 27. I think you're just coming into your professional career (at that age). At the time, South Melbourne had a lot of good players in all the lines so he probably went a little bit unnoticed, but not in our changing room.

"He was very well respected. You obviously don't make someone captain if you're not first on the team sheet, so he was always first picked on the team sheet."

What was Postecoglou's special quality as a coach?

Petersen said Postecoglou was a "hard-arse", his management style was a bit like "lead, follow or get out of the way."

Postecoglou didn't get a lot wrong, Petersen said. "I can say that, but I think his history shows it. He's managed to get it right on the big days. It's by design, it's not coincidence. He gets it right. You can read all the books in the world. And you have either got that gift, or you don't have that gift.

"A knee injury ended his career prematurely, so he turned straight to coaching. I believe he still would've coached but certain motivations came into play when he had to retire, so maybe he felt there was unfinished business.

"He was always a student of the game and I'm delighted for him (in his coaching career) because football is his life and Australian football will benefit immensely."

What of the early years?

"He was never one to go out, he was grooming himself for this at 20. We were going out to nightclubs and letting off a bit of steam, but he never did. He would go to the movies or go for dinner but he was always good company.

"He was always quiet and unassuming, but he has a wicked sense of humour when he wants to involve himself and he comes out with some classic one liners."

Having taken the South Melbourne job in 1996, one of Postecoglou's first big calls was to tell Petersen his career was over.

"He tapped me on the shoulder and retired me. It was an emotional time because I thought I still had something to offer and we were mates," Petersen said.

"But he was candid, honest and I appreciated that. It showed he took the job seriously and made decisions in the best interests of the club."

Years later at Spurs, Postecoglou's wicked sense of humour was still evident in some of his press conferences. Asked by a reporter after a match: "How did Sarr pull his hamstring?" Postecoglou replied: "Running mate! Something you and I don't do by the looks of it."

He had reporters scrambling for their keyboards in February 2024 when he started to answer a question about the January transfers outcome.

He began: "Probably the only disappointing one was yesterday. I thought there was a really good opportunity for us and, yeah, the club didn't feel it was the right move for us."

But he wasn't being serious. News that overshadowed football transfer speculation briefly was the switch of Formula 1 racing ace Louis Hamilton from Mercedes to Ferrari.

Postecoglou went on: "So, disappointed with that, but he ended up at Ferrari, so we just have to cope [with it]."

Looking at the journalists at his pre-match presser: "Oh, look at you all! You were ready to type away... Nah, it (the window) was a good one, mate, it was a good one."

> *"One of Ange's hugest strengths is recruitment and his attention to detail in the players that he gets for his way, the system and the way he wants to play."*
>
> **Socceroos coach Graham Arnold**

CHAPTER 26
THE ANGE EFFECT

Postecoglou became something of a street-art hero in his home town, Melbourne, with an outbreak of tribute murals.

In 2023, three passionate football fans turned Melbourne into "ANGE TOWN" creating giant posters of Postecoglou they put up in Hosier Lane in the city.

The six bigger than life-size works featured achievements in the career of Postecoglou, up to his appointment as head coach of Tottenham Hotspur.

The project was the brainchild of Dean Drossos, Peter Giasoumi and Dean Kotsianis,

Drossos told *Neos Kosmos* about how the project was conceived.

"I've known of Ange for the longest time – my dad used to be in the committee at South Melbourne, worked with the club back in the 90s when Ange was a player and a coach," he said.

"Then throughout the years, we've just kind of been watching his story and as soon as he went to Tottenham, Dean (Kotsianis) and myself kind of knew that we had to put something up of Ange, as kind of a mural and a way of showing our appreciation of what he's managed to accomplish over his 20 or so years as a manager."

It wasn't the first time Postecoglou was honoured with larger-than-life artwork.

There was something of a kerfuffle in 2016 when Nunawading City FC in the eastern suburbs of Melbourne had a mural featuring three football identities painted in their clubrooms. They didn't choose any of their own players.

Coach Nick Dimitrakis arranged for the painting of a mural featuring Pep Guardiola and Johan Cruyff, greats of the world game. The third face? Ange Postecoglou. The work was done by Anthony Samargis, an artist friend of the coach's son.

"A lot of people – high-profile ex-players – didn't believe Ange was in the calibre of Pep and Cruyff," Dimitrakis said. They thought it was embarrassing to even compare him to the other two. "But those three guys always think outside the square. They don't think like other people," was Dimitrakis's response.

The seeds for the idea of the mural were sown in 2008, when Postecoglou was running the "V-Elite" youth development program with Football Federation Victoria while also working as an analyst for Fox Sports.

When the "V-Elite" program was shut down amid funding cuts, Dimitrakis convinced Postecoglou to transplant it to Nunawading City, a fairly small club with no juniors at the time.

Nunawading cast itself as the "development" club.

The style of play the club adopted was possession-based and playing out from the back. Sounds familiar.

Postecoglou has been featured in yet another mural.

Professional artist Shaun Devenney from South Australia took it upon himself to create a work (street art) called "Big Ange" in 2022, to honour Postecoglou's success at Celtic. It depicts Postecoglou with the Scottish Premiership trophy and gold medal around his neck giving a fist pump to the Celtic supporters.

The street art was created in Coventry Street, South Melbourne, the suburb where it all began for Postecoglou.

"The mural came up better than expected," Devenney told *The Celtic Way*. "I had planned to do it for ages … I wanted to do something with regard to Ange.

"I tried to speak to South Melbourne – Ange's old football club – to see if they had a wall or anything like that but… there was too much paperwork and red tape to get it over the line. So I just went and did it off my own back.

"My Twitter feed went absolutely mental after I posted it. The notifications went absolutely nuts. I was hoping that Celtic would get involved and put it on their social media pages.

"I sometimes get commissioned to do murals through businesses or councils but I did the Postecoglou one off my own back. He needed to be immortalised with a mural in Melbourne.

"It became a labour of love and I think that is why it has come out looking so good."

Postecoglou put the writing on the wall for his rise to the lofty heights of the EPL in an interview in 2011 while he had charge of Brisbane Roar in Australia's A-League: "I always knew I'd be a good coach and I've always wanted to do things that haven't been done before, that make a difference. I'm determined to leave a mark, that's what drives me. There's not a moment when my brain isn't ticking over, it's 24-7. I can't help it if it's an obsession, I'm hoping it's a healthy obsession. To be honest, I feel like I've only scratched the surface. There's definitely more to come."

After success in Australia then Japan and Scotland, where to? Postecoglou knew he was destined to coach in the "big time". It was just a question of where? First thoughts of pundits were that his beloved Liverpool was a strong chance. Or maybe even Arsenal where he was thought to have shown interest in the Gunners' youth development program.

He went to Tottenham Hotspur. He had never really outwardly shown an inclination to go in at the top. His speciality since heading overseas had been taking a struggling club and getting it on an upwards trajectory. That certainly was the case in Japan and Scotland. Even back home in Australia with the Brisbane Roar where people eventually started calling the Brisbane team "Roarcelona", the success reminiscent of that achieved by Spanish team Barcelona, sort of.

Postecoglou may have moved on, but the master tactician remained a friend of Nunawading. Dimitrakis said the club could pick up the phone at any time for footballing advice.

Peter Cklamovski spent the best part of 16 years observing Ange Postecoglou at work – watching, listening and taking notes.

He was a member of Postecoglou's coaching staff when Australia won the 2015 Asian Cup.

Before then, the Sydney-born player had shown promise as a junior, most likely heading to the Australian Under-17 youth squad. A serious car accident put paid to those dreams.

He studied sports science at university and took his first job as a coach at the King's School. From there, he went to Westfield Sports High, and in 2004, he linked with Postecoglou – then in charge of the Joeys, Australia's Under-17s side.

He then followed Postecoglou into the Young Socceroos (Under-20s) set-up, through to 2007.

When Postecoglou couldn't find a job in Australia after being sacked from the Youth teams and joined third-division

Greek outfit Panachaiki in 2008, Cklamovski went with him.

When Postecoglou was "moved on", Cklamovski went his own way, returning to Australia to work as a fitness coach and analyst at Perth Glory and Adelaide United.

In 2012, the pair were reunited at Melbourne Victory where Cklamovski became the club's fitness coach.

From 2014 to 2017 he was an assistant coach for the Socceroos, working on an ad-hoc basis.

In the meantime, in 2016, Cklamovski had gained his Pro-license accreditation. He observed his coaches closely, particularly Postecoglou.

The two are of course different characters – "the Ying and the Yang", as Cklamovski described it – but there was considerable mutual respect and understanding.

Cklamovski did find his way into the Under-17 program eventually, appointed head coach of the team in 2017, for a year, before resigning.

He began his own overseas coaching odyssey in 2018, as an assistant coach to Postecoglou at Yokohama F. Marinos. In 2020 he was appointed head coach of Shimizu S-Pulse in Japan, a job he gained through his association with Postecoglou at YFM, J-League champions in 2019.

"I'm like a sponge, mate," Cklamovski once said. "I absorbed everything I could. I had the mentality, if I could push him and raise his level anywhere I could, then at the same time, I'm pushing myself to higher levels.

"And that was my mentality for years working with him, because I just admired how good he was – even when nobody else did.

"I've served a strong apprenticeship. I'd say, respectfully, I've learned from the best... his obsession with the football he wants to play, his belief and conviction within that is always powerful, never waivers away from it. His success that he creates is a byproduct of all of that. He's a serial winner, mate."

Cklamovski was the fourth coach from Australia to take the helm of a Japanese club – after Eddie Thomson, Graham Arnold and Postecoglou. S-Pulse was a defence-oriented team, and the Australian was brought in to re-build, to implement the attacking style that supporters wanted. Covid intervened and S-Pulse decided after the competition resumed under tight protocols in 2020 that they could do without Cklamovski.

In 2021 Cklamovski moved to another Japanese club, Montedio Yamagata in the J2 League. He saved the club from the prospect of relegation, climbing the league table to finish equal 6th on goal difference. The next year the club narrowly missed promotion.

His record with Montedio Yamagata: longest undefeated streak in club's history; longest win streak in club's history; highest win percentage of any manager in club's history; highest points per game of any manager in club's history.

Two years later, the 44-year-old Cklamovski was on the move again, into the top J1-League as head coach of Tokyo-based FC Tokyo that hadn't tasted premiership glory since 2011.

As Postecoglou began duty with Celtic, Cklamovski described him as a pioneer for all Australian coaches … "he continues to inspire everyone."

The move to Celtic was a great reward for his hard work over a long time – "He is at a club that suits him, a big club. He is one of the best in the world. Now he just needs to showcase himself to the world. He will turn Celtic around," Cklamovski said at the time. Prophetic.

Back at Nunawading City FC, the club remained in awe of Postecoglou, even though he didn't play or coach there at a senior level.

Ange's son James did play for the club. His coach at the time Steve Voursoukis told a club podcast in 2022 that "James had his dad's attributes. He was ruthless. He was a winner, he hated losing."

Voursoukis said it was an honour to have the national coach of the time watching his own son's games from the sidelines.

Another podcast panellist was former Melbourne Victory, Norwich (UK) and Brisbane Roar goalkeeper Michael Theo.

He described playing under Postecoglou: "There was plenty of structure, the team knew how we were going to approach the game, so everyone was on the same page and the bind we had in the whole group and the belief we had once we started getting results and rewards for our efforts." The results were three successive A-League premierships.

"It was amazing playing under Ange; his leadership, his knowledge of the game, tactically, he covered all aspects. For me it was a fantastic period," Theo said.

Steve Brimmer was a coach at Nunawading when Ange set up the junior program, before he became an A-League coach. Brimmer's son Jake (more recently a central midfield player with Melbourne Victory in the A-League) joined Postecoglou's program. Brimmer recalled Ange's philosophy of playing out from the back. "No matter what circumstances, you had to play the ball out from the back."

The Nunawading club's podcast panel honoured Ange Postecoglou as "an amazing coach," the panellists sitting below the mural of the three coaches, Postecoglou, Guardiola and Cruyff.

The Nunawading City FC's mission statement says: "Our core values are Respect, Leadership and Teamwork," mantras with which Postecoglou is familiar.

Postecoglou's involvement in junior development at the time was under the auspices of the Victorian Secondary Schools and Football Federation Victoria "V-Elite" youth development program.

Just down the road from Nunawading, Kon Kyranakis was heavily involved in the Box Hill United Football Club, as a player and later in coaching. He's still involved in coaching, as an assistant in the National Victorian State League Division 2 with Clifton Hill (premiers in 2023).

Kon's son Nick as youngster aged 7 or 8 attended one of Postecoglou's VSS "V-Elite" programs.

Nick went on to join the Melbourne City academy for three years before joining Nunawading senior team in the National Premier League Victoria 3 competition, one of thousands of Victorian football players who have experienced the expertise and influence of Postecoglou.

Even Kon attributes his own coaching style to what he has seen from Postecoglou: "Very influenced by Ange. First touch, keep, then move the ball."

FOOTNOTE; Pep Guardiola is the manager of EPL club Manchester City, He is the only manager to win the continental treble twice, the youngest to win the UEFA Champions League. He also holds the records for the most consecutive league games won in La Liga, the Bundesliga, and the Premier League. He is considered to be one of the greatest managers of all time.

Johann Cruyff was a Dutch professional football player and manager. One of the greatest players in history, and as the greatest Dutch footballer ever. Because of the far-reaching impact of his playing style and his coaching ideas, he is regarded as one of the most influential figures in modern football. He died in 2016.

Rick Mensink has met Ange Postecoglou several times over 30 years. Australian-born Mensink was a player at Ringwood from the age of 7 to seniors. He has coached at several clubs, including Box Hill and Richmond in the National Premier League.

He knew many of the people and players at South Melbourne, helping some transition from the club to their next phase, even finding new clubs though not in an official capacity.

How would Mensink sum up Postecoglou? "Ange is basically a great guy, obviously a great coach and manager, but also exceptionally humble."

Coach or manager? "He's an out and out coach and leader. Very good tactically and he knows how to put a good team around him. He knows how to achieve superior performance from his support staff and his playing staff."

Mensink noted that Postecoglou's success in Japan seemed to have been underrated.

"He went from Yokohama to Celtic. The J league is a

significantly better league than the Scottish League. Yes, Celtic is a big global brand, a big club," Mensink said.

"The J-league is a very serious league. Japan's national team is rated higher than the Scottish national team. The GDP of the J-League would be significantly more than the Scottish League and the standard unequivocally would be higher than Scottish football.

"It was seen as a big step for him going from Yokohama to Celtic. Historically, it is the fame of the name Celtic, its history and its strong connections to the EPL.

"Not many managers/coaches have come out of the J-League to go to the EPL. Frenchman Arsene Wenger came out of the J League (Nagoya Grampus Eight) to go to Arsenal in 1996 after a year in Japan. He became the club's longest serving and most successful manager.

"There's a plethora of coaches who have gone from the Scottish leagues to the English Premier League (Postecoglou among the latest), and back and forth.

"Ange is a purist. He has a very distinct style for the way and belief in the way he wants to play football. He is a coach. He excels in communicating the way he wants his team to play and everyone's role in the strategy."

Mensink said he believed time spent observing Arsenal's operations helped shape Postecoglou's entry into the EPL – "I think Ange had a look at the way Arsene Wegner conducted himself," he said. "Top clubs will open themselves up to a guy like Ange and show them the ropes basically. There's a real nurturing collaborative environment if you are at the right level."

Postecoglou also had spent time observing Manchester City as part of that club's extension programs with its affiliates, notably Yokohama in Japan while he was manager there.

MONEYSPINNERS

Postecoglou had a high regard for Japanese football: "Japan is obviously a more mature league," he said. "They've got more teams and more professional teams. They've got three professional divisions, promotion and relegation, the players earn a lot more money. Because of that, the quality of imports are a lot better because of the money. All the clubs are well funded and well supported. It's where you'd like to think the (Australian) A-League would be in 10-15 years' time and that is the challenge that lies ahead for the competition."

Mensink and Postecoglou crossed paths once when both were involved in suburban clubs.

Mensink said: "Ange actually turned up at Port Melbourne in a lower division at one stage when he was looking for a coaching role. He did try to pinch four or five of my better younger players at the time when I was at Bulleen/Essendon Royals.

"I was brought in to coach the Under-21s at Essendon Royals around 2007. (Royals merged with Bulleen a couple of years later).

"I had an absolutely outstanding group of Under-21s which I'd coached from Under-16s. The standout of that group was a young man called Matthew Leckie. There was another good pro, who went to South Melbourne called Bradley Norton and a couple of others.

"Ange went to Port. It's not on his CV. He definitely tried to take four or five of my best players. He got four of them. But he didn't get Leckie."

Ange did eventually coach Matthew Leckie; he was a member of the Socceroos team that won the Asia Cup in 2015.

CHAPTER 27
THE COACHES' COACH

Postecoglou's impact at Tottenham caught the attention of the football word, not just in the EPL or soccer.

Since 2007 America's NFL has played competition matches outside the US (where it is often referred to as gridiron), including the UK and Germany in Europe. UK games were played at Wembley until 2015 then Twickenham Stadium from 2016-17.

Tottenham's home ground Hotspur Stadium was used in 2019, then put on the NFL roster for 2021-29.

During the break for international EPL matches in October 2023, the NFL's Baltimore Ravens played Tennessee Titans at Spurs Stadium, the Ravens winning 24-16.

Ravens head coach John Harbaugh paid tribute to Postecoglou and the Spurs academy after spending a week there, training at the Enfield stadium complex.

Postecoglou and the American coach exchanged notes.

Harbaugh said after: "I really enjoyed Tottenham, when we practised over there. Just look at the facilities.

"I had the chance to talk to their various staff members. The Head Coach was amazing – I really liked that guy. He's really good with people. He really understands just how to motivate a team, how to build an organisation – he's done it in different places. I was just trying to pick his brains as much as I could.

"And then all the people around him... the performance people were pretty special. We got to see the young players. It was kind of cool seeing the Academy. That's different than us. We have High School and College. You guys have the academies and the clubs. Talking to those kids... they're kids, but they're really talented. So I learned how small our sporting world really is."

Harbaugh wasn't the only coach from outside the round-ball game to seek out Postecoglou and pick his brains.

In the world of the egg-shaped (sort of) ball of the Australian Football League, Hawthorn coach Sam Mitchell has been a keen observer of Postecoglou's rise.

Near the end of October 2023, he and assistant coach Adrian Hickmott spent a week with Spurs in the club's lead-up to a match with Fulham.

Mitchell also spent some time with Postecoglou in Perth in the EPL pre-season when Spurs played a "friendly" there.

Micthell, a Spurs fan, would be well placed to see how much things had changed at Spurs as he also spent some time there in 2019, before Angeball arrived. That trip was to spend time at the Spurs academy observing training, planning and allocation of resources for players in the sports science, medical and coaching areas.

Mitchell also spent time with Postecoglou while he was at Celtic in Scotland.

The game may be different but a lot of coaches from various football codes were becoming interested in how Postecoglou goes about getting his team to perform so well at elite level.

Even rugby league coaches were keen to tap into what Postecoglou was doing at Tottenham.

Brisbane Broncos (Australia's NRL) coach Kevin Walters, a friend of Postecoglou from the days when both were working in different codes in Melbourne, was another to call in on Tottenham Hotspur.

"It was a personal development tour where I went to see how other organisations work, their set-ups, coaching structures and sharing information around everything to do with our games," Walters said.

"Ange is a very good operator. His personality is probably the biggest thing that stands out for me, where he is humble about everything he does.

"Tottenham are one of the bigger clubs in the Premier League but Ange is not taking that for granted.

"He is working as hard as he has ever worked, he tells me, which is refreshing for us to hear because we are all working hard to get where we want to go too."

Both coaches were under pressure to produce results that fans craved – premierships of course.

"There are those expectations on our clubs and I spoke to Ange about that too," Walters said.

"He is certainly a realist and understands that you have got to put things in place and over time those structures pay off.

"He is new but very confident in the staff and roster that he has in place that he can do very well, as are we."

SHADES OF KANGA

Was Postecoglou inspired by legendary Hawthorn AFL Coach John "Kanga" Kennedy when he berated his troops at half-time in the Spurs match against Manchester City in a 3-3 draw in December 2023?

According to Dejan Kulusevski Big Ange was angry after the first half showing, telling players they were overthinking things. Spurs were down 2-1 at the break.

"The coach was angry with us at half-time – he told us to just play," Kulusevski said after the game.

Asked to elaborate on his team talk, Postecoglou said: "There would probably only be a few words I can say! Joking aside it was more trying to get the players to believe in themselves rather than anger at them."

Johnk Kennedy's "Don't think, do" half-time address to his players in a game against North Melbourne in the 1975 grand final is part of Australian sporting folklore.

Kennedy recalled: "It was half-time against North and we had a few academics in the side at the time and they were telling me what we should do and 'I think this' and 'I think that'.

"It just got too much for me so I just said, 'Don't think, do something!'

CHAPTER 28
A WAY WITH WORDS

*"He would have you so hyped,
I think it would have been unsafe to send us directly
onto the pitch after one of his talks.
We'd have been sent off after about 10 seconds."*

**Socceroo Jackson Irvine on
Ange Postecoglou's pre-match speeches.**

It is fair to say the Postecoglou's press conferences at Tottenham can be entertaining. And he likes to make sure what goes on the record is right.

After a 3-1 win over Bournemouth a reporter noted: "It's not just three points today, but it's three points that put you within a point of the top four."

Postecoglou: "If I'm not mistaken, we are three points off the top."

Football reporters noted that Postecoglou is not prone to the kind of outbursts they saw from his predecessor Atonio Conte – not given to regular rants or displays of rage as he patrols the sideline.

But that's not to say he isn't capable of laying down the law when he feels it is required.

In another press conference, Postecoglou faced persistent questioning about Eric Dier's future after not being selected for the FA Cup match against Burnley.

"He's injured," Postecoglou said. "He just pulled up sore and didn't train yesterday."

A questioner persisted: Was his absence linked to reports about him being traded to Bayern?

Postecoglou snapped back: "Separate issue mate but don't question my integrity. When I say he's injured, he's injured. He didn't train yesterday.

"It's got nothing to do with anything else." Dier, however, eventually, was sent out on load to Bayern.

It didn't take Postecoglou long to set some members of his Spurs squad straight on what was required of them, echoing his approach on the team bus back in Australia in 1996 when as an assistant coach of South Melbourne he took over the microphone and chastised players for their attitude after a loss.

Mr Nice Guy can quickly send a shiver down the spine of any "offender" who has stepped out of line. He is unrelenting in getting his players to do what he wants.

Hotspur's Dejan Kulusevski revealed Postecoglou launched into a furious half-time spray in a "friendly" against Ukrainian side Shakhtar Donetsk in a 2023 pre-season match after players seemed to let their guard down for a few minutes.

The score was 1-1 at the break and the Spurs players got a serious talking-to in the rooms.

Spurs went on to win the match 5-1.

Postecoglou also became furious with Pierre-Emile Hojbjerg during the match, shouting to him "Hojb, play. Play" from the sidelines as he directed players in the style he wanted. Kulusevski appeared to be unmarked on the wing but Hojbjerg passed back to Ben Davies.

As players at Celtic already knew, if you want to avoid the wrath of the manager, don't pass the ball backwards.

In a match between Celtic and Raith Rovers in 2021 Postecoglou was heard yelling at his players to stop passing the ball backwards.

He explained: "It's not about getting angry or having a blast just for the sake of it. It's about whether I feel something isn't as it should be. Usually it's around not so much the game or results, but behaviours. If I see a behaviour that I don't think fits in, I'll make sure the player and the group knows about it. That's my role. I can't ignore it or let it go and be nice. That's what everyone expects of me. If someone displays something that I don't think fits in, I'll have no hesitation in telling them it needs to be addressed."

Postecoglou also was known to tick-off a player for taking too long with a throw-in.

Incidents such as these don't suggest there's a dark side to

Postecoglou at all. They simply highlight his passion about getting teams to play the way he wants – commitment to Angeball.

It emerged that on the Spurs pre-season trip to Australia and Asia he gave one player a dressing down in front of the team.

The incident that provoked Postecoglou was something the player had said to medical staff. Commentators noted Postecoglou's desire to promote humility among his squad and to keep them aware of the privilege they hold as professional footballers and that no single player was any more or less important than another.

Yves Bissouma is believed to have been given the same reminder when he arrived late for pre-season training.

While Postecoglou was in charge of Celtic in 2022, former Brisbane Roar defender and captain Matt Smith was asked if Postecoglou got angry. "Yeah, he gets angry. He gets angry when you don't follow the principles.

"He doesn't care about making mistakes. If you make mistakes trying to do the right thing he'll praise you and support you, he'll back you one million per cent. If you start not being brave, not working hard enough, if you're cheating or cutting corners he'll be angry.

"He punched the whiteboard when we played away at Perth. We scored with the last kick of the half to make it 2-2. I remember him at half-time, all of a sudden he erupted about not moving, not showing, not adjusting, not being brave enough and hiding. Not doing what we had been doing week in week out.

"That's what makes Ange so passionate about his beliefs. If you stop doing that, the system breaks down. All the time you are doing that, it's like a wave, you keep riding."

Postecoglou's team talks can be something special, too.

Socceroo Jackson Irvine said his inspirational team talks got players really hyped up. Irvine told *talkSPORT*: "He used to do his team talks about three hours before the game, before we have even done the pre-match.

"Because, honestly, you get so emotional and so hyped up that you want to run through a bowl of spaghetti and stick your head in it.

"He would have you so hyped, I think it would have been unsafe to send us directly on to the pitch after one of his talks. We'd have been sent off after about 10 seconds!"

CHAPTER 29
SPEAKING OF ANGE

Celtic fans took quite a while to warm to the appointment of Ange Postecoglou as manager of their beloved team. He wasn't the appointment supporters originally were hoping for – certainly not the one they were expecting. They probably would never have heard of him.

That was probably the case with Tottenham Hotspur fans, too. At Glasgow, Celtic fans did their research and it wasn't long before 14,000 thousand of the club's followers had "liked" the news on Twitter.

One fan posted: "He's a class coach. Wins trophies playing exciting football."

Other posts: "Celtic have just secured 1000s of Aussie fans. We wish him luck. Looking forward to watching our greatest manager strutting his stuff at one of the world's most famous clubs." And "Won titles at pretty much every club he has managed. Took Australia to a World Cup and won Asian Championship."

Many fans had called for the appointment of Eddie Howe (manager at Newcastle) or another big-name coach with

European experience.

Some of the detractors: "A reckless gamble. Really the best we could get? Doubt it. Board embarrassing themselves again." And "I quite like the cut of the big guy's gib. Doesn't alter the fact he's a complete Hail Mary..."

In an interview with the *Celtic Star* (for Celtic supporters) in 2021, former Socceroo teammate Scott Ollerenshaw (then technical director for Sabah FC in Malaysia) was asked what made Postecoglou a good coach.

His answer: "So many things but I'll summarise...

- Incredibly high standards... and an ability to keep pushing his staff and players to keep getting better and never be satisfied. This means that every day they go into work with a hunger to keep getting better and better.
- An ability to get staff and players to buy into his methodology and buy into the project. This means that once they buy in, they are totally loyal to his methods and beliefs on how he wants his teams to play. Bottom line is a coach cannot coach unless his players want to play for him and will run through a brick wall for him.
- An ability to have total trust in his staff thus giving them the confidence to do their jobs without him constantly looking over their shoulders... I believe he delegates very well.
- An amazing appetite to keep learning himself and keep evolving as a coach. He has complete tunnel vision and will do it his way no matter what. Anyone who thinks

Ange is a yes man is totally wrong, he is the opposite of a yes man.
- His methods work. He is very attacking-minded, he makes progress up the pitch through combination play but as soon as they turn it over they will hunt and press as a pack to win it back ASAP. Always goals both for and against when an Ange team is playing. Fitness levels for Ange-coached teams need to be amazing. No luxury players."

The announcement after two years that Postecoglou was taking the job down south at Tottenham Hotspur drew a mixed reaction among the Celtic faithful.

After taking over at Celtic Park in 2021 and delivering great success, Postecoglou was worshipped by Hoops fans, not just for the silverware he collected but also for the way he embraced the culture of the club.

When his departure was announced, some fans criticised him for turning his back on the club.

An image on the official Celtic Twitter account of Postecoglou with the three trophies he brought to the club in the 2022 season, drew a more sympathetic response, some fans expressing how sad they were to see him go and thanking them for what he achieved.

Former Celtic striker Chris Sutton said: "I don't get the argument that he can't manage in the Premier League.

"Look at his track record, it speaks for itself. I think people would have sat up and noticed the job he's done at Celtic."

The news of his appointment at Spurs wasn't met with immediate enthusiasm there either.

Tottenham fans took to social media to express their discontent.

Even before the appointment was confirmed, some fans took to Twitter to launch #NoToPostecoglou in protest.

But you have to dig much deeper than often shallow social media posts to understand the high regard in which Postecoglou was (and is) held.

Spurs players certainly had a better understanding of what Postecoglou brought to the team.

Argentinian international and Atalanta defender Cristian Romero joined Spurs on loan in 2021 and transferred on a five-year deal for £42 million ($A 80 million) in 2022. But he felt he hadn't been able to give his best under managers Santo and Conte.

He told *football.London*: "After winning the World Cup, I came to Tottenham, and the group was a little separated from the manager, but I feel responsible for the poor season we had. I'm not happy that the season ended that way, and I'm readying myself to repay all the trust the club put in me, and I'll be working to give my best. The new manager has brought us renewed hope, the group is looking great right now, and we'll try to have a great season to propel Tottenham as high as possible."

Some EPL managers obviously were impressed with

Postecoglou's appointment at Spurs.

One who lauded the move was Manchester City manager Pep Guardiola.

They'd met in July 2019 when Postecoglou oversaw Japanese J1-League club Yokohama F. Marinos.

City and Marinos played a "friendly" which the English powerhouse won 3-1, but the Japanese club had 58% of possession.

"Another exceptional manager is coming," Guardiola said when he heard of Postecoglou's appointment.

"I was lucky to meet him in Tokyo years ago when he was manager at Yokohama, one of our clubs in the City Football Group, and it was an interesting chat.

"He did an incredible job (at Celtic), and he will do an incredible job for Spurs."

West Ham manager David Moyes, who got the better of Postecoglou (3-2) in the new coach's first match in charge of Spurs at a "friendly" in Perth, Western Australia in July 2023: "I don't need to give Ange any advice – that's for sure.

"His team played well enough that they could have easily scored more goals, and we were a bit fortunate that we didn't concede more."

Former Spurs boss Harry Redknapp believed Postecoglou was an ideal fit at Tottenham.

"I met him out in Australia, when I went out and managed the Jordan national team, he managed the Australian team.

"Tim Cahill played for the Australian team and I was just chatting to him before the game and he said 'our manager's fantastic'.

"I said 'really'? He said, 'Harry, he is top drawer' and that was it. I'd never heard of him at that time... Timmy Cahill said he was brilliant and that's stuck with me. Then I've watched how he's done at Celtic and he's been brilliant, I love him.

"There's no fannying (around) with him, he says it as it is, I like him."

Les James Murray AM was a Hungarian-born Australian sports journalist, soccer broadcaster and football analyst. He was presenter of the SBS television program *The World Game*. He died in 2017 and had known Ange Postecoglou well.

Murray first spotted Postecoglou as "an attacking player" in the mid-1980s at South Melbourne.

"He was very, very quick and he had a long mullet flying behind his head as he galloped up the field," Murray recalled.

He said that after Postecoglou took over as national team manager, the Socceroos went from "the bottom of the toilet" to a team that "made me very proud to be an Australian."

After Postecoglou's arrival at Spurs, the football media was particularly keen to find out more about him.

Targets of their inquisitiveness have been those who have played under his leadership.

Tim Cahill's comments are typical of the views many players have expressed.

"No-one would ever have said we'd have won the Asian Cup cause we're Australian and it's soccer. And we're not supposed to win. But that's what we've done. That's what Ange has done," Cahill said after Australia's success in the Asian Cup in 2015.

Former Brisbane Roar captain Matt Smith won back-to-back titles under Postecoglou. He said in a BBC interview that the coach was not content with simply winning, he wanted to "change the whole scope of how Australian football was perceived."

He said: "Ange's massive strength is his ability to be able to bring players along that journey and buy into what he does.

"There's zero tolerance for players that don't want to follow. We were never made to feel comfortable, we were always pushing to be better, always developing, always working harder than any group I've experienced before.

"It didn't matter if you were the biggest player in the dressing room or the youngest – if you weren't pulling your weight or following his principles, he was very ruthless.

"I always thought, 'He's looking at me'," said Matt McKay, who played under Postecoglou for the Socceroos and Brisbane Roar. "It was like the Mona Lisa (painting).

"Ange was probably the best coach I ever worked under. He made you go out on to that pitch and feel like no one could touch you," Socceroos defender Ryan McGowan said.

Celtic goalkeeper Joe Hart: "He is top, he is really, really good. He is really clear in what he wants and the biggest buzz for me is I am playing for someone who is pushing me and I am learning new things every single day.

"I'm an old dog in this game and the fact that I am having to do that and stay on my toes and still want more and trying to improve is a great feeling. It makes me feel alive."

Arsenal legend Ian Wright hoped Postecoglou would bring the Gunners' cross-town rivals the success that they desperately needed. "Ange has done fantastically at Celtic. He seems to be somebody that's a very cool, really calm character. I think it's fantastic for him to get the Tottenham job," Wright said.

Football Australia's CEO James Johnson said the appointment was good news.

"This appointment is a personal triumph for Ange and his family, and we are absolutely delighted for them," Johnson said.

"Ange personifies the Australian football story: a proud Greek-Australian who immigrated to Australia at a young age and found his place in a new Australia through football. After making a name for himself domestically, from his playing days at South Melbourne Football Club to his success as Socceroos' head coach leading the team to Asian

Cup glory in 2015 on home soil, Ange has gone on to test himself successfully in the global football arena against the world's best."

Between May and August each year, many clubs go on a pre-season tour to help keep the players in shape ahead of the upcoming football season and spread the EPL "gospel" to parts of the world that don't get a chance to see the glamour teams first-hand.

Spurs had mixed luck in their pre-season tour to Australia and South-east Asia. They lost 3-2 to Premier League rivals West Ham in Perth, their game against Leicester City in Bangkok was abandoned due to the weather and they defeated Lion City Sailors 5-1 in Singapore.

Their next pre-season (friendly) game was against 14-times Ukrainian champions Shakhtar Donetsk, to raise funds for Shakhtar's charitable foundation, Shakhtar Social, in support of the ongoing humanitarian crisis in Ukraine resulting from Russia's attack on the country, particularly the Donetsk region.

The Club made a financial contribution and an extra donation of nett proceeds from ticket sales to Shakhtar Social.

Spurs also distributed match tickets to displaced Ukrainian families in North London. Children from the families led the teams out as mascots on the day.

Ukrainian popstar Olya Polyakova performed her country's national anthem, accompanied by a visual tribute to the work being done to support those affected by the conflict. That included Spurs season-ticket holder Jon Dann, who been volunteering to provide humanitarian aid to Ukraine since the war began. He had co-ordinated and led eight deliveries of medical supplies that were driven from London across Europe and into Ukraine. He addressed the crowd at half-time.

The result of the game was a comfortable win for Spurs.

Spurs had one other game before their season-opener against Brentford, a visit to Barcelona on 9 August for the Joan Gamper Trophy, an exhibition match hosted annually in August by Barcelona, usually at Camp Nou, before the start of the new Spanish La Liga season.

The result was a 4-2 win for the home side.

Then it was down to the serious business for Ange Postecoglou and his charges as they sought to right the ship for the new manager's tilt at the Premier League and a return to European football.

There was one downside for Ange Postecoglou in his move to Spurs. He had to pull out of the fantasy Premier League group he was in with mates.

Speaking before the season-opener with Brentford, he said: "I've got a few friends coming to the match. It's fair to say I've been inundated for tickets but it's great because they've been along for the journey. We all had those dreams and we're all living it together because for me they're just part of it as well because I wouldn't be sitting here today without them.

"They're all going to be here and for the first time in I reckon 20 years I've had to pull out of our fantasy Premier League group as well which I'm gutted about and if they try to grill me for information they're getting nothing out of me. I don't need to play now because I am a Premier League manager. There you go, It's not a fantasy anymore!"

Postecoglou changes football teams. Football teams don't change him. "I am still Dad, I am still a husband, somebody's mate and that doesn't ever change," he says.

Postecoglou has been mindful of his young sons and the effect of his globetrotting on their lives, particularly how they speak.

He said he greeted his two youngest boys with an iconic "g'day" over breakfast each day.

He also has the hit Australian children's television show *Bluey* on repeat so his young sons don't forget their roots.

He told the *Australian Sunrise* television program: "It is a real battle. They spoke with a US twang (when at an international school in Japan while he was at Yokohama F. Marinos) and then developed a Glaswegian twang when we were in Scotland (with Celtic) – God knows what they will sound like after living in London."

At Glasgow, he said his family has adjusted well.

"I've got two young boys who go to school.

"We came from Japan and when you move away as a family unit you tend to really rely on one another when you go to live in a foreign land.

"The two boys (Alexi and Max) are really close as brothers because we have lived in Japan.

"Coming here was an easier adjustment. The language obviously helped and moving to Scotland has been great.

"My boys went to an international school in Japan where all the teachers had an American background so they had an American accent in Japan which annoyed the crap out of me.

"The great thing about kids is they adjust. As long as they have got a loving family unit wherever you take them they are fine. Kids are pretty resilient."

Eldest son James has been serving in the Hellenic Armed Forces on Lemnos, Greece.

CHAPTER 30
EARNING THEIR SPURS

Comparing players from one era to another is subjective.

Tottenham Hotspur FC has been around since 1882 when it was founded by members of the Hotspur Cricket Club in Tottenham.

How would you go about nominating the best 10 or 20 from the thousands who have pulled on the Spurs strip in that time? Different eras produced their own stars.

The late 1970s and 80s were good days for Spurs.

They were promoted to the England First Division in 1978-79 and finished 11th.

Keith Burkinshaw took over as manager in 1976-77 and the side was relegated to Second Division, and it took until the next decade for Burkinshaw to get the results that took Spurs back into First Division where he built a team that included Glenn Hoddle, and Argentinians Osvaldo Ardiles and Ricardo Villa.

Spurs won the FA cup in 1981 and 1982 and the UEFA cup in 1984.

Terry Venables took over in 1987 and the signings of Paul Gascoigne and Gary Lineker helped spurs win the 1990–91

FA Cup, the first club to win eight FA Cups. Hoddle became one of only 18 players to score 100-plus goals (110) for Spurs. Not bad for a specialist mid-fielder.

IN MEMORY OF EL TEL

Ange Postecoglou led Australian tributes to former England and Socceroos manager Terry "El Tel" Venables, 80, who died on the morning of the Spurs EPL match against Aston Villa on 26 November 2023.

Venables had been a Spurs player and managed them during his illustrious football career. Tottenham held a minute's applause ahead of its game against Aston Villa, with players from both teams wearing black armbands.

Venables was hired by Australia in November 1996, leading the Socceroos on an unprecedented run to the final of the 1997 Confederations Cup. He was in charge of the Socceroos for what probably was their most infamous match, late in 1997.

Chasing their first World Cup appearance in 24 years, Australia held a 3-1 aggregate lead over Iran with 15 minutes to go in the second leg of an intercontinental playoff. But after play was disrupted by a ground invader, the Socceroos lost momentum and gave up two late goals to lose the tie on the basis of away-goals. Venables described the game as "one of the saddest sporting moments of my life."

Postecoglou said despite the lack of success ("he almost

got us to the World Cup") and his short time in charge of the Socceroos in 1996-97, Venables had a significant influence on Australian football. "The biggest testament," he said, "is that anyone who I have ever come across that has worked with him will say he is by far the best coach, manager and tactician they have come across.

"If you are asking about a person who embodies everything this football club has always wanted to be, it is Terry. It wasn't just about the way he managed or coached, it was the person he was."

As a player, he won two England caps and made more than 500 club appearances between 1960 and 1975, largely for Chelsea, Queens Park Rangers and Tottenham.

He was manager of the England team from 1994 to 1996, most notably leading them to the semi-finals of Euro 96. He also managed Barcelona, winning La Liga.

The modern era at Spurs boasts players Harry Kane and Son Heung-min, the 31-year-old South Korean having been at Spurs since 2015. But trophy success eluded the team – nothing since the UEFA Cup in 2007-08.

Despite the lack of results, Kane continued his march up the all-time Premier League scoring table as he moved into second place on 6 May 2023. At that time, Kane had scored 213 Premier League goals in 320 appearances and was alone in second place, surpassing Wayne Rooney. It was unlikely he'd be challenging all-time leader Alan Shearer (260 goals in 441 appearances).

The 2022-23 season was Kane's 13th at Spurs, having played a total of 455 matches and scored 284 goals.

Another Spurs great of the recent era, also no longer at the club, is Welshman Gareth Bale.

Bale played as a winger at Hotspur and Real Madrid and was widely regarded as one of the best footballers of his generation and one of the greatest Welsh players of all time, best known for his explosive pace, athleticism, and powerful long-range shots on goal. He would have been well-suited to Angeball.

Bale joined Spurs in 2007, playing under Harry Redknapp from the 2009-10 season, mostly as a winger.

Go back a couple of decades and it would be hard to go past Jimmy (James Peter) Greaves MBE.

Greaves passed away in 2021. He was regarded as one of the greatest strikers of all time and one of England's best ever players.

He was England's fifth-highest international goal scorer with 44 goals, including an English record of six hat-tricks, and is Tottenham Hotspur's second-highest all-time top goal scorer.

Greaves was the highest goal scorer in the history of English top-level football with 357 goals. He finished as the First Division's top scorer in six seasons, more times than any other player.

He is also a member of the English Football Hall of Fame.

Other Tottenham legends include Dave Mackay, Glenn Hoddle, Robbie Keane, Gary Lineker, Teddy Sheringham, Pat Jennings, Ossie Ardiles... it's a long list and one that could be argued about forever.

What about the managers/coaches?

Bill Nicholson, probably Mr Tottenham himself, is long remembered as a hero at the club. Spurs' home ground until 2017 was White Hart Lane, in Bill Nicholson Way, High Road, Tottenham.

Nicholson joined Spurs in 1938 and was manager for 16 years. He was a permanent fixture around the club until his death in 2004.

His Spurs team became the first to win the League and FA Cup double in the 20th century, but he went on to add many trophies.

His philosophy of playing entertaining football defined the club that he helped to build.

A controversial figure among fans, Harry Redknapp turned spurs into Champions League contenders. Some of the greatest moments in the club's history came under Redknapp.

Spurs were bottom of the league with just two points from their first eight games in October 2008 when Redknapp was lured from Portsmouth, where he had built a team that won the FA Cup.

Redknapp's time at Spurs eventually unravelled, but he built an attractive, attacking team around some of the best players that have been seen at White Hart Lane. Players including Luka Modric, Rafael van der Vaart and Gareth Bale gave Redknapp's Spurs a competitive edge.

What was in store for Spurs under Ange Postecoglou?

At his first press conference in the job, he conceded he faced a big challenge in turning Spurs' fortunes around and urged players not to resist change as it "only derails the process."

His aim was to rebuild the team and do things "my way;" that would be Angeball, borrowing from the name afforded then new England cricket coach Brendon McCullum (a New Zealander) and his style of attacking cricket that became known as "Bazball."

Postecoglou was at Lord's watching the Australia-England Test match just before taking up the Spurs appointment.

He told Sky Sports: "I love Bazball mate, I think it's brilliant!"

"In any sport, when I see teams kind of break the traditional mould, that's when people get really uneasy about it – and that's when you know, 'OK, this could be something special,'" he said.

"It's not guaranteed to work. It could all fall to pieces and end up in tears. But when you make people uneasy and uncomfortable with what they see it probably means you're breaking new ground and I love that in anything in life.

"That's where the special stuff exists and that's the kind of space I'm in."

When asked if he should sacrifice his attacking principles in favour of a more conservative approach, he replied: "My view on that is, if you are a strict vegetarian, you don't drop into Macca's just because you are hungry mate, you know? This is what I believe in."

His players knew where Postecoglou stood.

One of the club's best finds in recent years was James Maddison. He explained the manager's approach: "If you look back at the teams he (Postecoglou) managed, they've always been front-foot pressing teams.

"The first day he came in he said pressing high is almost a non-negotiable at any stage of the game.

"We had a game in pre-season where we went 1-0 or 2-0 up and we kind of stopped pressing and sat in a little bit – and he went ballistic at half-time. It was Shakhtar Donetsk here (at Tottenham).

"He said that's almost how Tottenham have been in the past, trying to protect a lead. He said it's non-negotiable, keep going and keep pressing, and we go and score three and four."

Postecoglou's man-management style sees him happy to keep his distance from his players off the field, perhaps a hangover from his days in charge at South Melbourne when he had to tell mates they were no longer in the team.

"I don't think any of the players will ever say they got close to the gaffer. I would never sit down and have a coffee with them," he said. "I always like to keep a distance between me and the players. The biggest responsibility I have is to make decisions, and I want to make the best decisions all of the time.

"It's human nature if you like somebody, or maybe dislike somebody, that might affect you. I always keep that distance. I'd like to think the players always know I've got their back and I'll fight for them right until the end. I've always said to the players I take responsibility for all the bad stuff that happens and I think players appreciate that. They know where they stand with me."

CHAPTER 31
EYES ON EUROPE

Spurs had reached the Round of 16 of the European Champions League in the past two seasons before Postecoglou's arrival, winning only three of eight games both times.

Postecoglou had taken Celtic to the Group stage, so he'd have some idea of the level of play that was required.

Postecoglou certainly wasn't naive when it came to working out what needed to be done.

He qualified Celtic for the group stage of the 2022-23 Champions League for the first time since the 2017-18 season and followed up again for the 2023-24 season where Brendan Rodgers would replace the Australian. Rodgers was returning to Celtic, four and a half years after leaving mid-season to take charge of English club Leicester City.

Celtic had a tough start to its Champions League campaign in 2022, losing 3-0 (0-0 at half-time) to European giants Real Madrid in the first game of Group F at home in Glasgow. It was Celtic's first Champions League appearance after a five-year absence.

Postecoglou had promised his side would keep its attacking mindset, even against the 14-times winner of Europe's top club competition.

Celtic finished with one point from its four matches. After a 1-1 draw in Scotland against Midtjylland from Denmark, leading 1-0 until Socceroo Awer Mabil headed home an equaliser. Celtic bowed out 3-2 on aggregate, leaving them to contest the Europa League.

After the loss, Postecoglou acknowledged the fine margins in the Champions League.

"You know at this level you're not going to dominate the whole game, you get a certain amount of opportunities to punish the opposition," he said.

"Unless you experience it, it's probably the hardest way to learn but the best way to learn."

Celtic was knocked out in all three European competitions in 2022-23 – the Champions League, the Europa League and the Europa Conference League.

Disappointing for Celtic and Postecoglou but he had learned what was required to contend.

With his experience at Celtic still fresh in his mind, getting Spurs back into European competition would be a big task, but not impossible.

English teams have had mixed results in the Champions League finals; Manchester City defeated Inter Milan 1-0 in 2022-23 to become European champions for the first time, one of their three titles for the season.

Spurs' eighth place in the EPL meant they were well behind the four EPL clubs that qualified for the 2023-24 draw that involved 32 teams from throughout Europe.

Spurs reached the Champions League final in 2018-19, losing 2-0 to Jurgen Klopp's Liverpool in Madrid in the first all-England final of the championship. It was Spurs' most recent appearance in the Group Stage.

Tottenham was the first British club to win a major European competition, with the European Cup Winners' Cup in 1963. In 1972, they won the inaugural UEFA Cup and repeated the effort in 1984.

The team regularly qualified for European football in the 2010s. There were slim pickings for Spurs since their loss to Liverpool in 2018-19.

The European Champions League was founded in 1955 and was then referred to as the European Cup. It was re-branded in 1992.

The Champions League is the top tier of European club football; the second tier is the UEFA Europa League and the third tier is the UEFA Europa Conference League.

The Champions League format was to change for 2024-25, in response to a failed initial attempt to set up a rival Super League European (ESL) competition. Whether an ESL would get off the ground remained unclear, particularly after the European Court of Justice ruled in December 2023 that banning clubs from joining the league was unlawful, though noting that the decision did not mean a breakaway league would "necessarily be approved."

Postecoglou said the proposed European Super League was unlikely to become a reality, as fans didn't seem to like it.

"The response it got the first time around is a pretty good indicator of where it sits within the footballing fraternity in general," he said.

The main changes for the UEFA Champions League:

- The number of teams in the group stage will increase from 32 to 36;
- Each team will play eight games over 10 match-weeks instead of six games over six match-weeks;
- The group stage will be replaced by a single league table that will decide who advances to the knockout rounds; The initial phase will comprise one single league table that includes all teams;
- Each club will play eight group-stage games against different opponents, with four home matches and four away;
- The top eight will go through to the knockout stage; those from ninth to 24th will compete in a two-legged play-off to progress.

Similar format changes were applied to the Europa League (eight matches in the league stage) and Europa Conference League (six matches in the league stage). Both include 36 teams in the league phase.

For England's national team, qualification for UEFA's Euro 24 in Germany was the immediate priority in 2023.

The campaign hit a "speed bump" when Gareth Southgate's team took on Ukraine in Poland on 9 September, drawing 1-1. Southgate lamented after the game that the team's attacking play was not at the level he wanted.

Perhaps he should have had a chat to Ange Postecoglou. England did qualify for the Euro 24 play-offs.

CHAPTER 32

WE NEVER STOP

" You definitley cannot leave Spurs matches before the final whistle as anyhting can happen while the ball is rolling."

Fan on BBC's *Tottenham Fans Voice.*

What had fans seen from Postecoglou's Spurs in 2023?

According to one commentator: "A fine interplay of defensive mid-blocks, tight midfield, and ferocious counterattacks, all transitioning seamlessly on the pitch. The passing is short, and fast. The formations keep changing shapes."

The style of play was best summed up by one of Postecoglou's oft-used expressions, "we never stop, mate."

He told players at a training session: "Just get it into your heads: we never stop, we never stop. We'll stop at half-time, and then at the end of the game when we celebrate. But during the game we don't stop."

The philosophy probably wasn't more evident than in the EPL game against Brentford in February 2024. Spurs were down 1-0 at half-time. What Postecoglou said at the break wasn't recorded but when the second half resumed, Spurs put on three goals in just 8 minutes, going on to win 3-2.

Even seemingly down and out in a match, the attack was still alive. A late winner in a game against Brighton in 2024 took the tally of competition points earned by Spurs in extra time to 8, the most of any EPL team. Postecoglou's preferred starting formation (4-3-3) was expected to result in more Spurs goals, but his defenders would need to be up to the task of fluid and urgent movement around the pitch.

No surprise that his quickest players were the defenders, Udogie, Romero and van de Ven, the latter clocked as the fastest in EPl history with a dash back into defence at 37.38 km/h (23.22 mph) during a match against Brentford. Unfortunately, the trio all suffered from injuries in the first half of the season.

All-out attack and a rapid transition to defence was a "risk and reward" strategy. While Spurs to the end of January 2024 had scored 49 goals, only two fewer than Liverpool and Manchester City, they'd conceded 35, 16 more than Liverpool and 11 more than City.

Even after the 4-2 loss to Chelsea early in the season when the team was reduced to nine players, Postecoglou rejected the notion that he should have thrown everyone into defence.

Such an act of sheer desperation was not the Postecoglou way.

"It is just who we are mate," he said when questioned. "It

is who we are and who we will be for as long as I am here. If we go down to five men we will have a go," he said.

Recruiting became central to the strategy that Postecoglou stressed he wouldn't be changing.

A Spurs starting 11 going into the last quarter of the season, even the next season – assuming all players were available, and with newcomers included – could look like this: Vicario, van de Ven, Romero, Udogie, Draguson, Bentancour, Porro, Maddison, Kulusevski, Son and Werner. Something for fans to argue about of course. What of Richarlison, Hojbjerg, Sarr, Johnson and Bissouma, for example? A strong bench, as well.

But what format would suit best? A 4-3-3 formation was a preferred option, one also used by Manchester City and one of the most popular in world football for a long period. But Postecoglou added a twist.

In attack, Postecoglou reverts quickly to a 2-3-5 or 2-3-2-3 with his inverted full-backs joining the press. His defensive midfielder has the job of finding gaps in defence that can be exploited, but he must also be ready to drop back into a defensive line if possession is lost, something that would displease Postecoglou greatly.

The team Postecoglou was building had a distinctly youthful look.

Younger players that were given opportunities included Udogie, Sarr, van de Ven, Gil, and Skipp.

The Under-21s Development Squad (managed by Wayne Burnett) were facing relegation before the start of the 2023-24 season but were reprieved when the Premier League 2 format was changed. The young Spurs took up the challenge and were unbeaten in their first 10 games of EPL2, scoring 33 goals and conceding just 10 to sit on top of the 26-team ladder and six points clear.

As well, the club's Academy players were showing enough of their skills to warrant consideration in the seasons ahead, the Under-17 and Under-18 teams winning Premier League Cups in May 2023.

Some notable players began their Spurs career at the Academy including Harry Kane, Ledley King, Jake Livermore, Ryan Mason, Danny Rose, Andros Townsend, Kyle Walker-Peters and Harry Winks. All boasted international representation.

THE YOUNG ONES

Postecoglou has always been willing to give young players a chance. He did it when in charge of the Socceroos in the 2014 World Cup campaign.

2010 World Cup: Average age: 28.4 Average caps: 32.7 Aged 30 or over: 9 Players Aged 25 or under: 5 players

2014 World Cup: Average age: 25.7 Average caps: 17 Aged 30 or over: 4 Players Aged 25 or under: 14 players

During the 2023 calendar year transfer windows, Spurs didn't sign a player over the age of 26 among their seven recruits. The average age of their starting side in the early weeks of the 2023-24 season was 24.5, the third youngest in the EPL (behind Arsenal 24.1 and Burnley 23.5).

The club had its eyes on several youngsters for the future. They signed talented young Swedish central midfielder Lucas Bergvall the day he turned 18 on the last moments of the January 2024 transfer window. He was to join the squad in July.

Bergvall played his first game for his national team just months before signing with Spurs.

Another investment in the future was 16-year-old Croatian whiz kid Luka Vuskovic from the Hjduk Split club. While Spurs could not bring him to their squad until he turned 18 under rules applying after Britain withdrew from the European Union, they were pleased to sign him ahead of Manchester City, Liverpool and Chelsea in the EPL and even Paris Saint-Germain. Spurs intended to leave him at his Croation club, which in turn sent him to Polish club Radomiak Radom "on loan" for the rest of the season. He'd make the move to Spurs in 2025 on a contract believed to be worth £12 million ($A22.8 million) running to 2030.

Vuskovic played his first professional game just two days after his 16th birthday in February 2023, becoming the youngest player to score for the Croatian team, though he mostly sat on the bench or played for the Under-19s.

He looked to be a good fit for Angeball – as a defender he scored six goals in 14 games for his Under-19s team.

Spurs already had Argentinian youngster Alejo Veliz on their books, signing him as a teenager. In January 2024, aged 20, he was sent out on loan to Sevilla (Spain) for him to gain more game time and challenge for a regular spot in Postecoglou's attacking line the next season.

Spurs Academy players would also come under notice for senior spots.

Antonio Conte hadn't seemed interested in bringing players into his squad through the academy. Postecoglou put his stamp on youth development where the young players were being skilled in using a 4-3-3 formation and Angeball, as were the Under-18s and Under-21s.

Spurs have four teams in elite level football: Premier League, Women's Super League, Under-21s and Under-18s. The latter two youth teams operate through the Spurs Academy. Spurs have Under-16 and Under-17 teams in its development centres.

The Under-21s play in the Premier League 2 competition that replaced the Under-21 Premier League from 2016-17. Teams can field an "over-age" goalkeeper and up to five other "over-age" players.

Under-21 players can play in club Premier League teams. (For the 2023-24 season, Premier League 2 comprised 26 clubs with Category One academies contesting a single division).

Spurs chairman Daniel Levy believed Postecoglou would restore the bond between the first team and the club's academy. That meant Angeball would filter down through the club to create a playing style for seasons to come.

"One of the reasons why we asked Ange to become our manager is that he believes in the academy," Levy said. "The relationship between the first team and the academy is really important. This is a club where we as fans get a great thrill out of seeing a player coming out of academy and into the first team.

"We want to see that flourish and I think that over the years we've got some very good players in our academy, and we'll see them coming into the first team."

Tottenham Hotspur Football Club Academy (Category One status) develops talented young footballers from the age of eight to 23 years. It employs a team of staff to identify, recruit, coach, develop and support about 205 talented young players.

How Tottenham Hotspur rated
(as at 2023-24 season start)

- 3rd highest English all-time average attendance figure.
- Joint 3rd most successful side in all time FA Cup history

with eight wins.
- 6th most successful side in all time League Cup history with four wins and four runners up.
- Joint 4th most successful English side in UEFA European competitions by trophies won (3).
- 10th richest club in world as ranked by Forbes.
- 12th highest income in world as ranked by accountancy firm Deloitte.
- The highest number of players to represent England (78).
- Highest number of goals scored by players representing England (255).
- 14th (joint) in number of English league titles won.
- 6th in ranking of all time major honours won by football clubs in England (26).

The records

- The first club to win the "Double" of the FA Cup and Top Flight Championship in the 20th Century (1960–61).
- Most consecutive League victories from start of a top flight season: 11 (1960).
- Most victories in a League season: 31 out of 42 games in 1960–61.
- Most Premier League goals scored by a player in a calendar year: 39 by Harry Kane in 2017.
- Most points in Division 2 season: (2 points for a win): 70 (1919–20).

- The only non-league club, since the creation of the Football League in 1888, to have won the FA Cup (1901).
- The first club to win the League Cup at the New Wembley (2007–08).
- First team to concede 1,000 goals in the Premier League.
- Most goals scored in a Premier League game: 9 (joint record).
- Most prolific goal scorers out of any English team in European football competition, scoring an average 2.1 goals per game.
- The first British club to win a major European competition – European Cup Winners Cup (1963).
- The first British club to win two different European Trophies – European Cup Winners Cup and UEFA Cup.
- British record of eight consecutive victories in major European competition.
- Most matches played in the UEFA Cup / UEFA Europa League by a British club.
- The first ever English club to win a UEFA competition (European Cup Winners' Cup, 1963).
- The first club to win the UEFA Cup (1972).
- The first team to score two or more goals in every UEFA Champions League group game (2010–11).
- The joint biggest winning margin in a UEFA competition final: 5-1 vs Atletico Madrid (European Cup Winners' Cup, 1963).

CHAPTER 33
THE CHANGE HAS COME

Two managers in the English Premier League changed the face of the game.

Pepe Guardiola has been at Manchester City since 2016, the year Ange Postecoglou published his book, *Changing the Game*.

Guardiola established himself as one of the great football coaches. His emphasis on possession football brought about 11 domestic league titles in 14 years.

The Spaniard, formerly at Barcelona and Bayern Munich, joined Manchester United legend Sir Alex Ferguson as the only two managers to have won Premier League crowns in three consecutive years. Ferguson's career and impact on the game has been well documented; a legacy of success, innovation, and leadership.

With Guardiola in charge of Manchester City, spectators see players in constant motion when the ball is "live". The principal has been called "positional play." It gives the impression players have free reign to do whatever they want. But that's not the case at all.

It is all about putting players into positions where

opponents are outnumbered.

Go back to 2016. Playing out from the back was the "thing", the game plan that set Manchester City apart from top league rivals.

That's pretty much what Postecoglou had been doing at the top level of football, whether it be in Australia, Japan, Scotland or now with Tottenham Hotspur.

A journalist wrote: "Postecoglou is not your typical EPL manager."

It would be difficult to say what a typical EPL manager is. Postecoglou is his own man of course, shaped by his experiences from when he was a five-year-old migrant lad to the times he spent winning championships at various clubs.

That story is the evolvement of Angeball, a game where keeping possession and scoring goals is paramount.

It isn't a case of Postecoglou copying Guardiola. Postecoglou's attacking methods can be traced back to his pre-teen days when he watched soccer on TV with his dad in their Melbourne home and seeing the joy on his father's face when a goal was scored. It was all about goals.

That was the first seed of Angeball, no doubt.

Today, the traditional perception of positional play is hard to recognise as defenders play out from the back. It may look frenzied and unstructured but it is well-planned. If the execution is right, the goals come.

As a player, Postecoglou was a noted defender. But he had

form in front of goals, too. Scoring goals remained at the forefront of his coaching philosophy.

The numbers worn by players are not necessarily indicative of their position on the field these days. But "back in the day" when the traditional formation was 5 in the forward line, 3 in the midfield, 2 backs and a keeper, the numbers represented these positions: 7 and 11 were wingers, 8, 9, and 10 were the forwards (9 usually over the ball for kick-off then in front of goal), 4, 5 and 6 the halves, 2 and 3 the full-backs and 1 was the keeper's number.

That formation is rarely seen these days, overturned by tactics that put everyone in the frame for attack, particularly in Angeball. While 9 might still be a striker, 10 is more likely to be an attacking mid-fielder, 2 and 3 can be seen pressing forward through the midfield and even 1 can be playing up the ground as his teammates go on the attack.

Some of the more famous number 10s have been attackers – Cruyff, Maradona, Pele, Zidane, and in modern times, Mbappe, Messi, Kane and Rashford. They are goal scorers. At Spurs, the No. 10 is James Maddison, replacing Harry Kane. Maddison is not of the Kane mould; Kane was an out-and-out goal-scorer.

Nevertheless, Maddison's value to Spurs was becoming obvious. Until an injury in the game against Chelsea on 6 November 2023 sidelined him for several months, Spurs reached the top of the EPL ladder with 10 wins in their first

11 games in which he played.

Resuming in the starting 11 in the game against Brentford on 31 January 2024, Maddison had 110 touches, 81 passes with an accuracy of 91.4%, his best stats for the season showing how sorely he was missed for the two months he was out.

He was going to be a key figure for the rest of the season and beyond.

Maddison's position at Spurs could be described as attacking midfielder, a floating No. 10, with an emphasis of creating opportunities. He says of his game: "I'm a player who loves to be on the ball and that fits with how the manager wants his players to play."

Postecoglou: "He's the kind of guy that when the ball gets to his feet, things happen. He also works hard for the team. He embraces that side of it."

Postecoglou thinks the days of the traditional No. 10 playing predominantly in attack have gone. These days the No. 10 has to attack and defend.

"With Madders, we need him to work hard defensively, and he's embraced that side of his role," he said. "He understands for him to continue to play and have an effect he needs to do both sides of the game. Just being good at the offensive side of the game, very few teams are going to carry those kind of players."

Maddison scored three goals and provided four assists before injury took him out of the line-up until late January 2024.

He played a key role in setting up the "overload" on opposition defenders when the attack began out of defence.

It is often difficult to see what formation is in play even from set pieces.

Before 2021-22, 4-3-3 was the third most preferred formation. It became number one for several teams that season. It is especially suited to teams that have wide forwards who can provide goals, and box-to-box midfielders.

In 2021-22, Jurgen Klopp (Liverpool) started all 38 matches with that format. It was also popular with Roy Hodgson (Crystal Palace, 82.3% of the time), Patrick Vieira (Chelsea, 76.3%), Pep Guardiola (Manchester City, 73.7%) and Eddie Howe (Newcastle, 66.6%).

The formation is not necessarily constant throughout the game. Far from it, as Spurs have shown.

Postecoglou explains: "I think if you look at my career, I play different formations. A lot depends on the players you have at your disposal and I've got this place in terms of football where I just think set formations are not quite a thing of the past, but there's such fluidity in football these days, especially at the highest level like the Premier League, you really need players who are able to perform multiple functions and roles within the side.

"For the most part I've played a 4-3-3 but you probably couldn't pinpoint many moments in the game where that actually exists. It's more about movement and space. For me the key thing will be to have a really good look at the playing group and see what strengths they have and then come up with a formation that brings the best out of them."

The role of playmakers cannot be overstated. Postecoglou refers to the "classic" players in that role, Maradona, Cruyff – "guys who would do things that maybe others who would look at the game a little differently."

He also singled out Paul Gascoigne at Spurs (92 appearances from 1988-92) – "the players who when the ball arrives at their feet, people genuinely get excited because its in the player's nature to look for something that's going to be creative and hurt the opposition… they're the kind of players I like… especially in the midfield… they're exciting on the ball, lively with their feet."

While taking Australia to the 2014 World Cup Postecoglou used an attacking 4-2-3-1 formation, based on a back four comprising two central defenders and two full-backs. Two deeper central midfielders operated ahead of the back line. Further forward, an attacking midfield trio played behind a centre-forward.

A key player in that set-up was Tim Cahill, an attacking mid-fielder who could also prove lethal in attack, particularly with his skill in the air from set pieces or crosses from the wings. Cahill played for Millwall and Everton in the UK.

Another key player in Postecoglou's World Cup campaign

in 2014 was Mile Jedinak, signed as an assistant at Spurs in 2023. The tactic of Jedinak and Cahill holding their positions in the midfield allowed the full-backs to take an attacking role – Angeball 101.

In 2015 Postecoglou began to adopt the 4-3-3 format – four defenders (who could attack from the deep), three midfielders, and three forwards.

He used it in the Socceroos' 2015 Asian Cup success and in more than 80% of his matches in two years at Celtic.

In the Socceroo campaigns of 2017 (Confederations Cup) and 2018 (World Cup qualification) he would switch to a 4-4-2 format when in attack. A strong attacking mid-field was effective but the players had to be ready to defend, too.

He reverted to the 4-3-3 formation at Yokohama F Marinos for their J-League championship in 2019. There he tended to keep his wingers out wide, creating a bit more space for his full-backs to become creative through the middle.

This format better suited his emphasis on retaining possession and attacking from well back. He has shown willingness to be flexible, however, using different formations to suit his purposes as attack evolves.

A pre-season "friendly" against Pep Guardiola's Manchester City in Japan saw a glimpse of the possession game that would be evident from the Postecoglou-coached Spurs in the EPL four years later.

His Yokohama side had 58% of possession and although

they lost 3-1, they tried to match Guardiola's own game plan, using a determined press and a high defensive line.

Yokohama had five shots on target and out-passed City by 607 to 455.

At Celtic, Postecoglou employed similar tactics. When three fullbacks formed the defensive line, one pushed forward as the attack built, bolstering the mid-field from where the goal-scoring opportunities could begin from the forward press. Possession was the dominant focus.

That might be an oversimplification of the tactics; the circumstances at different stages of the game would dictate variations.

What did Spurs think Postecoglou would bring to the EPL?

The theory of 4-3-3 is that it provides a balanced approach to attack and defence, wingers playing a crucial role in creating width and the midfielders providing support in both phases of the game. This allows teams to have multiple passing options, create overloads in central areas, and press high up the pitch.

What was evident was that if they were behind on the scoreboard, even going into extra time, Spurs were not out of the game.

Postecoglou explained further how his game plan works after a win over Bournemouth.

It was about players finding space and swapping roles to

create an unpredictable attack, even from the team's own goal line; disrupt the defence of the opposition, draw defenders away from the lines the attacking players could use.

"They've all got freedom," Postecoglou said. "We're very structured, but hopefully it doesn't look that way.

"Our structure is fluid because guys understand as long as there's movement out there, they're looking for spaces and other guys are filling the spaces they leave, then it doesn't really matter where they pop up or where they go. But there is a discipline within that; it's not about running anywhere; it's about going into the areas we work on constantly, and if it looks fluid, that makes us harder to stop."

Clubs such as Manchester City and Spurs now recruit players based on versatility rather strength in a specific position relating to a (nominal) number on their shirts. Yes, Spurs might have been looking for a centre-back or a midfielder, but they had to be more than that. They had to be centrepieces in defence and attack.

Guardiola may have started changing the game, Postecoglou is taking it to a new level.

But would that put Spurs in the frame for honours in 2024? Would he change his tactics when things went against the team?

"The scrutiny will come but internally, the players and the staff will see I'm not changing. This is who we are going to be," he said in a Spurs podcast.

"Yes, we're under-manned, yes we are going to have some key players missing but we are going to go out there, whether it's Aston Villa, Manchester City or whoever and we're going to play our football.

"I've got men out there who totally believe in something and for me that's gold because that's the biggest part of the battle. Being ourselves, playing our football, we can still get to where we want to."

No matter how dire the situation (no pun intended as Eric Dier was sent out on loan to Bayer Munich) as players became unavailable, Postecoglou remained bent on all-out attack, even from the deep.

A third-round win in the FA Cup over Burnley resulted from a stunning goal by Pedro Porro, his first for the season. Porro is a right-back or right-wing-back in the Spurs Lineup. By the FA Cup game, he had led Spurs in assists.

Another player to figure in Angeball was defender Emerson Royal who was developing into a centre-back from his regular position at right-back. "I'm very happy to play in this position, I've discovered that maybe it could be a position that ends up becoming one of my official positions," he said.

Postecoglou's record suggests most success comes in his second year.

His titles with South Melbourne, Brisbane Roar and Yokohama all came in his second year in charge. But he was well aware of what was expected of him at Spurs.

"I… understand at this football club I can't go three, four, five months without results because I won't last. That's the reality of it. If you measure on outcomes, yes, this looks like this has been smoother than the others. But I can assure you this has been just as challenging, if not more challenging because of the stakes here in the Premier League."

Success in the last quarter of the 2023-24 season would much depend on the return from injury and international duty of key players plus the addition of the "new blood."

Getting back van de Ven, Bentancur and Maddison was going to be vital. It was no coincidence their absence towards the end of 2023 put Spurs under stress, dropping games they should have counted as likely wins.

The January 2024 transfer window saw the first real moves to consolidate the new way for Spurs under Postecoglou. And it was all done through some astute dealing.

There was a new face within the team's scoring armoury. Timo Werner's assignment would be goals, alongside skipper Son. Richarlison finding form again also would be a plus for Spurs up front (he obliged with a goal in a 2-2 draw with Manchester United and two in the 2-2 draw with Everton).

Down the back, the defenders would be joined by Romanian Radu Dragusin brought in from Genoa for 13 million euro (and Djed Spence going out to Genoa on loan).

Both recruits made their debuts for Spurs in the 2-2 draw at Old Trafford, Werner recording an assist and Dragusin coming off the bench. Both had only a couple of training sessions before the match.

Postecoglou: "Getting Radu Dragusin in early was great. Getting Timo Werner in early was also excellent for us. The beauty of getting them in early is that they've already made a contribution."

The draw with MU pleased Postecoglou, his team having been hit with illness before the game and still with key players injured. The upside was a return earlier than expected of van de Ven, Bentancur and Romero.

The MU result kept Spurs in the top five of the EPL ladder, having lost only one game in their past six (four wins).

Postecoglou: "The only reason we're in the position we are is because we've had players who are prepared to put aside whatever adversity we're going through and give everything they have."

Players do that for Big Ange.

Werner and Dragusin were seen as a good fit for Angeball, complementing Maddison, van de Van and Vicario who moved to North London in the (northern) summer transfer window.

That gave a bright new look to the Spurs line-up. Would it be good enough to produce a top 4 or 5 finish in 2023-24 and at least a return to European football?

CHAPTER 34

'WE'VE GOT OUR TOTTENHAM BACK'

The five years leading up to 2023-24 had been a great disappointment for the Tottenham Hotspur faithful.

Under a succession of "big name" managers and head coaches, fans had seen inconsistent performances and uninspiring football.

Teams were even accused of "throwing in the towel" when behind, giving rise to the "Spursy" chant.

What was wrong?

The rot seemed to set in after Spurs lost the 2018-19 Champions League final 2-0 to Liverpool in Madrid.

That loss by itself, disappointing as it was, shouldn't have been enough to plunge the club into the downward slide that saw it miss out on all European competition in the 2023-24 season.

A succession of big-name managers – from Mauricio Pochettino and Jose Mourinho to Antonio Conte – couldn't apply the brakes.

Spurs crashed out of the Champions League in 2019-20 with a 4-0 aggregate loss to RB Leipzig in the Round of 16.

Mourinho was the manager then.

Their performance in the Premier League in 2019-20 (sixth) saw them drop down to the Europa league in 2020-21 and eliminated in the Round of 16.

They finished seventh in the 2021-22 Premier League season and entered the newly formed UEFA Europa Conference League where they were eliminated in the Group round, failing to reach the knockout stage. Nuno Espirito Santo was in charge until November 21, having been appointed in June. He was replaced by Antonio Conte.

Spurs returned to the Champions League in 2022-23 after finishing fourth in the EPL in 2021-22. They reached the Round of 16 where they were eliminated by Milan. Conte left in March 2022, replaced by Stellini who in turn was replaced by Mason.

Spurs recent record in the EPL: 2018-19 – fourth; 2019-20 – sixth; 2020-21 – seventh; 2021-22 – fourth; 2022-23 – eighth.

After the loss to Liverpool in the Champions League final in Madrid, the pundits were saying it was time for Spurs to "replenish, rebuild."

The 6-1 loss away to Newcastle in the EPL in April 2023 hit Spurs hard. The players were so embarrassed they offered to reimburse fans the cost of their tickets to St James Park.

"As a squad, we understand your frustration, your anger," the players said in a joint statement. "It wasn't good enough.

We know words aren't enough in situations like this, but believe us, a defeat like this hurts.

"We appreciate your support, home and away, and with this in mind we would like to reimburse fans with the cost of their match tickets from St James' Park.

"We know this does not change what happened on Sunday and we will give everything to put things right against Manchester United on Thursday evening when, again, your support will mean everything to us.

"Together – and only together – can we move things forward."

What could Spurs do to turn things around? Fans were becoming impatient. Their team had a new massively expensive state-of-the-art stadium. They didn't have a manager for 2023-24. The team's captain and leading goalscorer Harry Kane was rumoured to be leaving. There was no competition in Europe for Spurs. Some management personnel had been banned from the sport.

Could things get any worse?

Then, the club announced Ange Postecoglou had been recruited from Celtic in the Scottish League to take charge of Spurs.

You could almost hear the text messages buzzing around – "WTF?"

Spurs already brought in a new goalkeeper in Guglielmo Vicario for 2023-24, as well as England international James

Maddison and winger Manor Solomon.

Postecoglou's first press conference promised to be a lively affair.

"I'm delighted to be here," he told the mass of media at Hotspur Way. "I'm looking forward to the massive challenge ahead which I was well aware of before taking on the responsibility. I'm looking forward to working with the players and staff and being part of a really strong competition.

"From the outset, what's important is that we try to establish some sort of key principles of who we want to be, first of all. Not just in the way we play, the way we behave, the way we train, the way we interact with one another, the way we interact with everyone else. Let's see where that takes us."

Cynics might have called that a "motherhood" statement.

But what else could he say?

His focus was to get the team ready for the arduous 38-game EPL competition that lay ahead. And, maybe, a run in the FA Cup, although that didn't end well.

Asked if fans would need to be patient in his early days at the club, Postecoglou responded: "I don't know if it's about patience. You can't ask (emphasised) people to feel a certain way or dampen expectations. I think what I've tried to do wherever I've been, including Celtic, is allow them to form their own opinion based on what they see, not what I say."

As the EPL season moved into full swing, there's no doubt

football followers were amazed by what they saw.

One English football reporter noted: "It is unbelievable to think that Tottenham ended last season with an interim manager, without European football to look forward to and then lost their talisman (Kane) in the summer."

With a new management team in place in the latter part of 2023, the task became focussed on recruiting, short- and-long-term. There was no sense of "job done" after initial success.

Asked if he would like a substantial amount of money to spend on new signings, Postecoglou said: "Not necessarily. I've always said I've never felt it is about just spending money. That's been proved time and time again.

"If you get it all right then you've got a pretty strong case, but there's always a limit to every team. You can't have 24 world-class players. That will never work. It's been proven that it doesn't work.

"It's about having a squad that's balanced, guys that are committed to a cause. Having guys that maybe aren't going to play every game, but every time they play they are going to make a huge impact for you because they buy into what you are trying to build.

"Just spending endless money to get the best players has been proven that it is not the answer. The answer is to get the right chemistry in your team."

On the eve of the January 2024 window opening,

Postecoglou again indicated the club's recruitment would be about strengthening depth rather than collecting big-name signatories at premium prices.

He said "nothing magical" was going to happen in the January transfer window. That could have been a red herring, as the recruitment of German forward Timo Werner on a loan from RB Leipzig in the Bundesliga with an option to buy at the end of the season was considered a master stroke.

"The way we play takes a fairly hefty physical toll more than the way other clubs play," he said. "The way to sustain that and be a team, it's no secret we need a strong squad, we are nowhere near that at the moment."

Recruitment was not focussed on covering immediately for the raft of injuries. "Each window gives an opportunity to strengthen and grow. It's nothing to do with the injury situation; it's to do with building the side," Postecoglou said.

Some assistance to Son and Richarlison up forward was going to be ideal. That came early in the January 2024 trade window when Spurs signed Werner. Werner had Premier League experience with Chelsea in 2020 to 2022. If there was a criticism of his play it was the number of off-side calls against him. No doubt Postecoglou could convert that eagerness into an asset in Angeball.

Another major gain was Dragusin from Genoa in Italy. The 21-year-old Romanian was a central defender who could give Spurs some strength in defence as well as attack from the deep. Spurs beat Bayern Munich to his signature through to 2029-30.

New technical director Johan Lange, a former player, manager and coach, had been busy since his appointment in October 2023 looking at free agents and the asking-price he could expect for the players that fitted the Angeball mould.

Spurs would replace some players who knew they were on the outer by the amount of game time they'd had – their future would be elsewhere or at least they could go to a team where they could advance their cause with more valuable game time.

The transfer window also allowed for the recall of some players while others could be sent out on loan (some for a second time) or leaving on free transfer.

There was no massive spending spree to rival Chelsea's estimated £1billion ($A1.9 billion) outlay since May 2022. Compliance with EPL spending rules was essential.

Postecoglou still believed his team remained in the mix for the EPL title, well aware that Liverpool and Manchester City would be the teams he'd have to overcome, most likely when he came up against them towards the end of the season.

"We had four games when results went against us, but we've clawed our way back. We're still in there," he said. "Our performances for the most part have been pretty consistent, but all that is meaningless if we don't finish the season stronger than the first half of the season and that's what we've got to do."

Regardless of trades, the way forward for Spurs was definitely Angeball. There'd be no turning back.

Spurs were bright in attack and stoic in defence. A breakout from the backline was always on the cards. The fans rose when they saw a defender with the ball at his feet and moving forward, along with the rest of the team.

Look what he achieved with almost half his squad unavailable at times. Imagine what he could do with a full list available.

Postecoglou had changed the culture at Tottenham Hotspur in just six months. The fan base that was in the doldrums in the middle of 2023 was singing a new song in 2024. They were loving Big Ange.

None were more delighted about what was happening at Spurs than chairman Daniel Levy: "We're seeing football we used to see, that's all we want. All staff at the club, playing, non-playing, we're in it together. There's a different atmosphere around the place.

"We've got our Tottenham back."

If there was to be no glory in 2023-24, fans would be tuning in eagerly for Angeball in 2024-25.

After all, as Ange Postecoglou once said: "Everywhere I've been, the second year is where I've felt like the team has really taken hold."

EPILOGUE

*"Everyone's been very kind to me and
really supportive because they can see what
I'm trying to do but they don't leave me
guessing about what the objective is, but that's fine
because that's what you want –
you want passionate supporters and it's right our
supporters feel that way, but I can't let that
dictate what I do because I know what I need to do
to take this football club to where it needs to be.
It will not come from the joy of a one-off.
I know that it would probably be good
for me if it happens. It would be great for me,
but it's not what I'm interested in.
I'm interested in taking this club to a level
where it has success on a regular basis."*

Ange Postecoglou, January 2024

ANGE, FOR THE RECORD

Date of Birth: 27 August 1965
Pace of birth: Nea Filadelfeia, Athens, Greece.
Parents: Jim Postecoglou, Voula Postecoglou (later Postekos).
Sister: Liz.
Arrived Australia: 1970 (age 5).
Schools: Prahran State School, Prahran High School.
Married: Spouse Georgia. Children: James, Max and Alexi
First club: South Melbourne Hellas (age 9).
Playing position: Defender. Ten seasons at SMFC from 1984 to 1993. Left fullback. 193 League games, 19 League goals. NSL Championship winner 1984 (player) & 1991 (captain). 2000 Sam Papasavas Award winner.
Youth career: 1978-1983, South Melbourne.
Senior career: 1984-93 South Melbourne - 193 appearances, 27 goals.
1994 - Western Suburbs (4 goals)
International career: 1985 Australia U20s - 13 appearances, 1 goal
1986-88 Australia Socceroos - 4 appearances, 0 goals.
Tactical strength: Most commonly associated with a 4-3-3 format.
Team trademarks: Dominating possession, fluid movements and short passing style.
EPL debut match: v Brentford (away) 13 August 2023. Drawn 2-2
First EPL win: v Manchester United (home, Round 2) 19 August 2023. 2-0.

INDIVIDUAL HONOURS
National Soccer League Coach of the Year: 1997-98.
Australian Sports Medal: 2000.
PFA (Professional Football Association, Aus) Manager of the Year: 2010-11.
A-League Coach of the Year: 2010-11.
PFA Manager of the Decade: 2015.
AFC Coach of the Year: 2015.
Scottish Premiership Manager of the Month: October 2021, January 2022, February 2022, March 2022, April 2022, August 2022, September/October 2022.
PFA Scotland Manager of the Year: 2021-22, 2022-23.
SFWA Manager of the Year: 2021-22, 2022-23.
Football Australia Hall of Fame inductee: 2022.

THE EPL

The English Premier League competition is played between August and May with 20 teams playing each other home and away over 38 rounds and a total of 380 matches.

Three points are awarded for a win, one point for a draw and none for a defeat. The team with the most points at the end of the season wins the Premier League title. There are no play-offs.

Red and Yellow cards: Two yellow cards shown to the same player within the same game results in a red card and the player must leave the field immediately.

Cumulative yellow cards can result in suspensions. Five yellows accumulated before match week 19 results in a one-match ban; Ten yellows accumulated by week 32 will result in a two-match ban; Fifteen yellows by week 38 means a three-match ban; Twenty yellows in a season can result in the Regulatory Commission punishing the player in a manner deemed to be most fitting.

Penalties for instant send-off red cards vary according to the offence. For a sending off, after a second yellow in one game, the suspension period is one match. For a so-called professional foul, a player will also receive a one-match ban. If the foul in question is dissent, it will normally be a two-match ban. For violent conduct, the punishment usually is a three-match ban.

In the Premier League, managers can also get yellow cards. If they receive a second yellow in the same game, they will have to leave the technical area that is allocated to club officials on the sidelines. Four yellow cards in the same season will result in a touchline ban, eight yellows mean a two-match ban.

What's in a name? The name "Hotspur" can be attributed to Sir Henry Percy (1364-1403) whose family inhabited The Black House near where the Tottenham football club's stadium was built many centuries later. Sir Henry was known as "Harry Hotspur." He fought in several campaigns against the Scots in the northern border and against the French during the Hundred Years' War. The nickname "Hotspur" was given to him by the Scots as a tribute to his speed in advance and readiness to attack. Early "Angeball." The Tottenham Hotspur FC club was founded in 1882 and its emblem is a cockerel standing on a football.

Postecoglou Coach/Manager record to 6 June 2023 (pre-Spurs)

Team	Nat	From	To	Record				
				G	W	D	L	Win %
South Melbourne	Aus	1 Jan 1996	31 Dec 2000	160	85	33	42	53.13
Australia U20	Aus	1 Jan 2001	20 Feb 2007	34	23	4	7	67.65
Panachaiki	Gre	12 Mar 2008	22 Dec 2008	33	16	9	8	48.48
Whittlesea Zebras	Aus	18 Apr 2009	15 Aug 2009	16	2	4	10	12.50
Brisbane Roar	Aus	16 Oct 2009	24 Apr 2012	84	42	24	18	50.00
Melbourne Victory	Aus	26 Apr 2012	25 Oct 2013	32	15	7	10	46.88
Australia	Aus	23 Oct 2013	22 Nov 2017	49	22	12	15	44.90
Yokohama F. Marinos	Jpn	1 Jan 2018	10 Jun 2021	161	79	31	51	49.07
Celtic	Sco	10 Jun 2021	6 Jun 2023	113	83	12	18	73.45
			Total	680	365	136	179	49.56

SOURCES OF INFORMATION

Hellenic Museum, Melbourne ("Through a Child's Eyes"); *The Age of Ange* ABC documentary for *Australian Story*; Socceroos.com.au; Football Australia; South Melbourne FC; Keep Up, digital platform of Australian Professional Leagues; Celtic FC; *Sporting News*; *WeAreTottenhamTV (wattv.co.uk)* - YouTube channel for fans; *Neos Ksomos* Melbourne media; Tottenham Hotspur FC; English Premier League; *football.london*; *The Athletic*; sportbible.com; ozfootball.net; Players Voice; Au.soccerway.com; various newspaper interviews and reports in Australia and Europe, Tottenham Hotspur and Postecoglou press conferences, and Trove records. Transcript sources: ASAP Sports, Keepup.com.au, ABC. Other sources: interviews, as noted in text.

Ange Postecoglou books:

Changing the Game. Ange Postecoglou with Andy Harper. Penguin Random House, 2016.
Never Stop: How Ange Postecoglou Brought the Fire Back to Celtic. Hamish Carton, Pitch Publishing Ltd. 2023.